THE ECONOMICS OF CONSERVATISM

MARCELO PESCI

ISBN: 1481200240
ISBN 13: 9781481200240

Library of Congress Control Number: 2012923371
CreateSpace Independent Publishing Platform
North Charleston, SC

To Liberty, Prosperity And The Rule of Law

Almost from its beginnings the Conservative party had been pitifully weak in its grasp of economics.

Burke has possessed an admirable mastery of the subject and Pitt had understood finance; but except for Huskisson and Herries; to the latter years of Salisbury's government, economists had been Liberals and the Liberals had trounced the Conservatives repeatedly in this field.

As the old Liberals succumbed to the theories of socialism, the need for a conservative economics was desperate.

RUSSELL KIRK

TABLE OF CONTENTS

PREFACE

In the wake of the 2007 financial crisis, people wanted answers. How did this happen? Who is accountable? Will this happen again? True to form, government and the media made certain the public got those answers — answers that were simple and readily accepted. Sadly, the answers the public were given were not just simple, they were also unquestionably, absolutely wrong. *The Economics of Conservatism* is a no-holds-barred critique of political economy, written in response to the inadequacies and hyperbole of the economic analysis being presented to the public, and equally being peddled to investors.

This direct and urgent plea for a different point of view on economics and politics provides a detailed assessment of what we are doing, why we should stop doing it, and what we should do instead. In the process, the book touches upon the thinking and writings of four of the most influential economists of the modern age: Adam Smith, David Ricardo, Karl Marx, and John Maynard Keynes. With a didactic tone and an unapologetically conservative bent, *The Economics of Conservatism* guides readers through a series of arguments and offers analysis of the current state of economics, revealing an approach that is no longer part of the mainstream curricula.

The Economics of Conservatism starts from the premise that politics and economics are not separate sciences, and that economics — as we think of the field of study today — is not so much a science, but a tool of social engineering. Worse yet, the theoretical separation of politics and economics has thoroughly wreaked havoc in the thought process and analysis of those revered minds who were charged with the task of providing objective advice to policy makers. Fortunately, by looking to the spirit and the letter of the words of the great minds of economics and conservative thought, there is clarity and purpose that will allow us to extricate ourselves from our present situation in the hopes that liberty, prosperity, and the rule of law may be preserved and expanded for future generations.

The Economics of Conservatism is an inspiring and transformative tract that addresses fundamental questions: What is conservatism? What is economics? Who are our friends and who our foes in the world of economic ideas? And what we should be on the lookout for? It is an engaging book brimming with ideas — and even a few immodest proposals — that is certain to instigate a "revolution" of conservatism, at least in the hearts and minds of its readers.

INTRODUCTION

When I started writing this book back in 2008, in the darkest hours of the financial crisis, I was angry.

At the very moment when clear, level-headed, evaluation of the situation was most needed, experts appeared seemingly out of nowhere to peddle policies that they knew, or ought to have known would not bring with them renewed prosperity.

The verdict from the economists, the media and the political class was unanimous: the deregulation of the 1980s had gone too far. Regulation was too lax, and taxes were too low. We have had too much capitalism. It was time to come back to our senses and take our cue from John Maynard Keynes, even Karl Marx.

Never mind that exorbitant taxation and suffocating regulation were the most likely culprits.

Never mind that the financial services industry —largely blamed for the crisis— was the most heavily regulated industry on Earth.

Never mind that the most reckless and incompetent bankers had been heralded as heroes by the political class whose interests they had furthered.

People wanted simple answers, and they got them. Sadly, for every complex human question, there is always an answer that is simple, is easy, and is wrong. There wasn't a single soul even attempting to explain what was actually going on, why, or how it came to happen. Or how to make sure it did not happen again.

The sad truth is that very few people knew what was going on, including the why and how of it all. The economy had collapsed under the weight of a government that had grown too large, unwieldy, and burdensome for the economy to support.

Across the developed world, the state had outgrown its economic foundations and had crushed them to pieces.

Every politician knew however, that this was a once-in-a-lifetime chance to pass legislation that was dear to their supporters but at odds with public interest; so that it could be enacted only when no one was watching; *never let a serious crisis go to waste:*

a. Multitrillion-dollar bailouts of bankrupt institutions
b. Reckless debasing of the currency (robbing people of their savings)
c. Steep increases in public borrowing (thus taking away the future of the younger generation)
d. Steep increases in taxation (ensuring ever weaker recoveries)
e. Socialized medicine (saddling the country with yet another tax on jobs)
f. Direct presidential intervention in the manufacturing industry to favor special interests (rewarding reckless trade unions and setting an appalling example)
g. Flaunting of central banks' legal frameworks across the world (destroying a reputation that had taken decades of hard work to build)
h. Ignoring and bypassing international treaties (introducing a degree of mistrust in public authorities and legal instability theretofore unknown in the developed world)

And there are many more items in the legislation, all guaranteed not to resolve the crisis but to pave the way for even deeper crises in the not-too-distant future, and these crises will be used to justify more taxes, inflation, and government control.

We have been conditioned for two generations to expect the government to do everything necessary to help the economy, and no politician in his right mind would get in the way of all this "beneficence." Professional economists could have and should have. But we did not. The question was why?

Politicians repeat what economists tell them. The economists in turn repeat what they read in their books and just as Keynes had told us almost a century earlier:

> The ideas of economists and political philosophers, both when they are right and when they are wrong, are more powerful than is commonly understood. Indeed the world is ruled by

little else. Practical men, who believe themselves to be quite exempt from any intellectual influence, are usually the slaves of some defunct economist.

Economics had long ceased to be what it was meant to be: "*a branch of the science of a statesman or legislator with the twofold objectives of providing a plentiful revenue or subsistence for the people and to supply the state with revenue for the public services.*"

As we know it today, economics is not a science but a tool of social engineering:

By pulling the economic levers, economists, thinkers, planners, politicians, and even Hollywood stars believe they can mold, even *create*, the type of society and the type of individual they envisage as ideal—a society that is more often than not one that looks, thinks, and behaves just like the economists, thinkers, planners, politicians, and Hollywood stars in question (or, more precisely, an idealized version of themselves).

The economic levers are many and extremely powerful:

- Who is (or is not) allowed to do what
- Who is (and who is not) allowed to profit and by how much
- Who is made rich and who isn't
- Who is allowed to accumulate wealth and who has his wealth taken away
- Who receives loans, contracts, and government licenses
- Who is and who is not requested to pay such loans back
- Who pays taxes and who receives handouts
- Which activities are favored and which ones are not
- Which individuals and groups are showered with government money
- Who is expected to live under the law
- Who is, for all intents and purposes, immune from prosecution

This is not a comprehensive list of the tools at the disposal of the professional economist, but it gives you an idea as to why anyone who wants to *make the world a better place* will draw from this powerful arsenal first and foremost.

Some people may say: surely, we all want to do an honest day's work for an honest pay, a house, a family, a car, a pet, some security in retirement, and a fair chance in life for our children.

You may well think that way, but to the economist, those things imply a specific type of society. And she is right. And she may or may not like that specific type of society (in the case above, meaning a free, prosperous, capitalist society).

Contrary to popular belief, we do not live in a post-ideological world. We are more ideological than ever, but this time, instead of one monolithic doctrine at a time, we are presented with a myriad of single-issue ideologies whose only commonality is their contempt for that specific type of society I've just mentioned.

The purpose of this book is to provide the reader with the theoretical tools to identify and to counteract the threats to our liberty, our prosperity and the rule of law and more precisely, the threat to our economic freedom, because —as Margaret Thatcher so eloquently put it a generation ago— it is on our economic freedom that *all our other freedoms depend.*

It is widely believed that politics and economics are separate and largely unconnected;

That individual freedom is a political problem and material welfare an economic problem;

And that any kind of political arrangements can be combined with any kind of economic arrangements.

Such a view is a delusion.

MILTON FRIEDMAN

CHAPTER 1

CONSERVATISM AND ECONOMICS

First things first: What do we mean by conservatism *and what do we mean by* economics?

CONSERVATISM

Russell Kirk wrote,

"Conscious conservatism in the modern sense did not manifest itself until 1790 with the publication of 'Reflections on the Revolution in France.' In that year the prophetic powers of Edmund Burke fixed in the public consciousness, for the first time, the opposing poles of conservation and innovation*."

Conservatism is not an economic theory; it is a way of life *that is tried by experience and sprung from our condition*. A way of life includes, by necessity, the economic arrangements necessary to sustain it.

Edmund Burke told us,

If civil society be made for the advantage of man, all the advantages for which it is made become his right; it is an institution of beneficence, and law itself is only beneficence acting by rule.

- Men have a right to live by that rule.
- They have a right to do justice as between their fellows, whether their fellows are in public function or in ordinary occupation.
- They have a right to the fruits of their industry and to the means of making their industry fruitful.
- They have a right to the acquisitions of their parents.
- They have a right to the nourishment and improvement of their offspring.
- They have a right to instruction in life and to consolation in death.
- Whatever each man can separately do, without trespassing upon others, he has a right to do for himself.
- He has a right to all which society with all its combinations of skills and force can do in his favor.
- In this partnership all men have equal rights but not to equal things.

He that has but five shillings in the partnership has as good a right to it as he that has five hundred pounds has to his larger proportion. But he has not a right to an equal dividend in the product of the joint stock."[1] [2]

The conservative does not oppose economic leveling (the enforced equalization of living conditions) per se: "How far economic and political leveling should be carried is a question to be determined by recourse to prudence"[3]

He simply denies that any individual or group of individuals have a "right" to the fruits of the industry of others. In other words he denies that there is such thing as the right to enslave.

The so-called economic rights ignore the two essential conditions attached to all true rights:

a. The capacity of individuals to claim and exercise the alleged right.
b. The correspondent duty that is married to every right.

---

[1] Russell Kirk, *The Conservative Mind*

[2] Edmund Burke, *Reflections on the Revolution in France*

[3] Ibid.,

If a man has the "right" to what he has not earned (for example, to have his below-average income equalized toward the average), someone who has managed to make herself more valuable to an employer than the average—be it through training, experience, or simply by working overtime—will have the fruits of her additional effort confiscated so that her income can be "equalized" downward.

If a man has the right to a job, someone somewhere must have the duty to start a commercial operation for the sole purpose of employing him.

What's more when we use the word *rights* to mean "desires" or "wishes":

> The mass of men must feel always that some vast, intangible conspiracy thwarts their attainment of what they are told is their inalienable birth-right, thus fixing upon society a permanent grudge and frustration which can and will surface from time to time and corrode any real progress which may have been attained.
>
> The true rights of men, then, are equal justice, security of labor and property, the amenities of civilized institutions, and the benefits of an orderly society. (Russell Kirk)

Deliberate economic leveling may be necessary from time to time, and such a need should be determined by expediency.

A systematic redistribution of income ("redistribution" being a misnomer, since income was never *distributed* in the first place) amounts to an economic and then a societal suicide. Those who exert themselves lose any reason to continue to do so, while those who do not are handsomely rewarded.

But, most importantly, the capital needed to maintain what we already have and to create the businesses (and with them goods, services, jobs, opportunities, and tax revenue) of the future will be gone forever, and along with them, any hope of a decent life for the younger generation.

Depriving the younger generation of any hope —which is what *redistribution of wealth* boils down to in practical terms— for the benefit of another generation is a curse to the conservative who sees society as a "partnership between those who are living, those who are dead, and those who are to be born."

Politics and economics are not independent sciences: they are the manifestation of a general order and that order is *moral.*

Kirk, echoing F. J. C. Hearnshaw, tells us,

1. On many prudential questions, and on some general principles, conservatives may disagree from time to time among themselves, yet the folk called "conservative" join in *resistance to the destruction of old patterns of life,* damage to the footings of the civil social order, and the reduction of human striving to material production and consumption.

2. An abstract rigorous set of political dogmata: that is an *ideology,* a *political religion* promising the terrestrial paradise to the faithful, and ordinarily that paradise is to be taken by storm. Such a priori designs for perfecting human nature and society are an anathema to the conservative who knows them for the tools and the weapons of coffeehouse fanatics. The conservative *abhors all forms of ideology.*

3. Men not being angels, a terrestrial paradise cannot be contrived by metaphysical enthusiasts; yet earthly hell can be attained readily enough by ideologues of one stamp or another.

4. For the conservative, custom, convention, constitution, and prescription are the sources of a tolerable civil social order.

5. To general principles in politics —as distinguished from fanatic, ideological dogma— the conservative subscribes, these are principles arrived at by convention and compromise for the most part and tested by long experience. Yet these general principles must be applied variously and with prudence, [with] humankind's circumstances differing much from land to land and from age to age.

6. "What it all comes down to, is that a conservative knows that two plus two always, invariably, equals four, a fact of life that a liberal, on the other hand, is not quite willing to accept."

Kirk provides us with "six canons of conservative thought" (which he, in turn, draws from F. J. C. Hearnshaw's *Conservatism in England*):

1. Conservatives believe that true politics is the art of apprehending and applying the Justice which ought to prevail in a community of

souls (defining society as a "community of souls" and the state as its embodiment stands in stark contrast with Milton Friedman's take on the matter "to the free man the country is the collection of individuals who compose it").

2. Conservatives feel affection for the proliferating variety and mystery of human existence as opposed to the narrowing uniformity: egalitarianism and utilitarian aims that Robert Graves calls "logicalism" in society. A sense that *life is worth living*

3. Conservatives believe that civilized society requires orders and classes and rejects the notion of a "classless society": If natural distinctions are effaced among men, *oligarchs fill the vacuum*. Equality before the courts of law are recognized by conservatives, but equality in condition means equality in servitude and boredom.

4. Conservatives believe that freedom and property are closely linked: Separate property from private possession and the State becomes master of all. Economic leveling is not economic progress.

5. Conservatives distrust economists and other power-hungry innovators who would reconstruct society upon abstract designs.

6. Conservatives recognize that society must alter, for prudent change is the means for social preservation. Change is a tool of social preservation, not an end in itself.

Echoing Hayek's observation that there are "socialists in all parties," it is obvious from the above list that there are conservatives in all parties.

Who are and have been their opponents since 1790, and what do they believe?

Again we resort to Professor Kirk for guidance. He identified at least five major schools of thought that have competed for public favor since Burke entered politics:

- The rationalism of the "philosophes"
- The romantic emancipation of Rousseau and his allies
- The utilitarianism of the Benthamites
- The positivism of Comte's school
- The collectivistic materialism of Marx and other socialists

In a hastily generalizing fashion, Professor Kirk gives us the beliefs that, with varying degrees, run through the radical mind:

- The perfectibility of man and the illimitable progress of society called meliorism. Radicals believe that education, positive legislation, and alteration of environment can produce men-like gods. They deny that humanity has a natural proclivity toward violence and sin.
- Contempt for tradition. Reason, impulse, and materialistic determinism are severally preferred as guides to social welfare. Formal religion is rejected, and various ideologies are presented as substitutes.
- Political leveling. Dislike for old parliamentary arrangements and an eagerness for centralization and consolidation is present.
- Economic leveling. The ancient rights of property, especially property in land, are suspect to almost all radicals; all collectivistic reformers hack at the institution of private property.
- A rejection of Burke's concept of society as "joined in perpetuity by a moral bond among the dead, the living, and those yet unborn"—that is, the community of souls.

ECONOMICS

The word "economy" was formed by combining the Greek root *oikos*, meaning "house," and the ending *nemein*, meaning "to manage or control" and representing the art (or science) of managing a household, or more precisely, the expenses of a household.

This means that we (a person or household) earn some, spend some, save some, and invest some, and we constantly adapt our behavior to actual or expected changes in our financial circumstances and our environment to ensure we remain fed, clothed, and housed until we depart from this world—hopefully due to old age and not for the lack of food, clothing, or housing.

Anything beyond that is *politics*—that is pertaining to the preservation, organization, and administration of the state. Politics with numbers is still politics.

Known as "political economy" until the nineteenth century, its name was shortened to "economics" to imply a separation between the science and the political environment or the political interest of the economist in question.

In fact, such separation never took place and never will, for reasons that will become clearer as we delve further in this book.

It is widely believed that any kind of political arrangements can be combined with any kind of economic arrangements. Such a view is a delusion.

This subtle rebranding has profound implications. By dropping the qualifier *political*, the uninitiated will be under the impression that economists actually speak for a science of sorts, that they are—or at least are trying to be—objective, and that they have the best interests of the public in mind in the same way that we expect a physician to be scientific, objective, and conscious of her duty toward her patients.

Sadly, in the field of economics, nothing could be further from the truth. The change implied something more: the time of free people living in a free community was over. The country (and over time, the planet) had become a household with the government as dad, Social Security as mom, and the rest of us living in eternal childhood. There was no need to differentiate the economy of a household and the economy of the nation. The nation had become a household.

There are several classifications of the (apparently) distinct elements of economic analysis and practice:

- Microeconomics, which examines the behavior of individual households and firms, markets, and their interactions.
- Macroeconomics, which examines the above but encompasses the whole country or region under study.

Another broad distinction occurs between

- positive economics, which is a description of things as they are, and
- normative economics, which concerns itself with things as they *should* be, according to the economist writing the book or giving the lecture.

It is interesting to notice that, for many people, the terms *positive economics* and *microeconomics* are largely interchangeable. The same goes for *normative economics* and *macroeconomics*.

Morals can be defined as of or concerned with the judgment of the goodness or badness of human action and character.

A *moralist* is often defined as a person who seeks to regulate the morals of others or to imbue others with a sense of morality.

Let's keep these definitions in mind, because —with dismaying regularity— those who sought to regulate the morals of others or to imbue others with *their* sense of morality, have resorted to political economy, that is the control of the nation's purse strings to achieve their aims.

Thinkers of great fame and acclaim have provided us with working definitions of economics or political economy. Some of them are listed below.

Adam Smith defined it as "a branch of the science of a statesman or legislator with the twofold objectives of providing a *plentiful revenue or subsistence for the people* and to *supply the state with revenue for the public services.*"

Practitioner: statesmen. Objective: ensuring individual *and* public well-being

John Stuart Mill defined economics as "the science which traces the laws of such of the phenomena of society as arise from the combined operations of mankind for the production of wealth, in so far as those phenomena are not modified by the pursuit of any other object."

Practitioner: scholars. Objective: improving our understanding

Alfred Marshall provides his own definition along similar lines: "Economics is a study of man in the ordinary business of life. It enquires how he gets his income and how he uses it. Thus, it is on the one side, the study of wealth and on the other and more important side, a part of the study of man."

Practitioner: scholars. Objective: improving our understanding

Adam Smith is often called the "father of modern economics." John Maynard Keynes is often referred to as the "father of macroeconomics." It's obvious from the above text, and we shall see in more detail in subsequent chapters, that Adam Smith is not just the father of modern economics, but also a macroeconomist in his own right.

In this book we will analyze in some detail, the works of four economists which I consider the *fountainheads*, the sources of our understanding (and misunderstandings) in the field of economics: Adam Smith, David Ricardo, Karl Marx and John Maynard Keynes.

Smith was concerned with ensuring "plenty." Ricardo gave up "plenty" to concentrate on "efficiency." Marx gave up "plenty" and "efficiency" to concentrate on "equality," while Keynes gave up all three to concentrate on "keeping people busy."

And this pretty much sums up the *evolution* of economic thinking between 1776 and 2013.

Since it is obvious that an impoverished and desperate population would give conservatism a very short shrift, conservatives aspiring to public office should familiarize themselves with the writings of those economists, whose main purpose was the *promotion of plenty* for both the individual and the state. This is simply because in the absence of prosperity; liberty and the rule of law will go out of the window.

Whatever a politician wants to do with her country, she will resort to an economist to accomplish it. The economist, in turn, will draw from one of the *fountainheads*.

WHY DO CONSERVATIVES HATE ECONOMICS?

The battle is for the hearts and minds; the economy is just a tool.

If macroeconomics and normative economics are largely interchangeable in the mind of the economist, macroeconomic management becomes an exercise in morals, it follows that those who are unhappy with the way humans actually are will take a keen interest in the subject. And it should come as no surprise that the field has been dominated successively by liberals and socialists. Conservatives are nowhere to be seen.

Eighteenth- and nineteenth-century liberals saw the free economy as a means to move away from traditional morality, family, church, community, nation, and a sense of duty; to the creation—for lack of a better word—of a perfectly selfish (but enlightened) individual whose only duty would be the pursuit of (his own personal) happiness unhindered by morals, family ties, religious devotion, sense of belonging, patriotism, or any expectations of transcendence.

Socialists reacted to all this moralizing materialism by seeking to place themselves, not as an example to their inferiors, but as arbiters of society. The socialist intellectual turned politician, economist, or bureaucrat totally devoid of selfishness would seek to take from those fortunate enough to have and give to those unfortunate enough to have-not in a never-ending cycle of redistribution.

Both true liberalism and modern liberalism (socialism, or communism in European parlance) are *materialistic* ideologies. For them humans are nothing more than producers and consumers of things.

And these humans pursue their aims *individually*, as in the case of true liberalism or as *class warriors* as in the case of modern liberalism.

Neither ideology concerns itself with the survival of the nation, the conservation of life and culture nor, indeed, with any human aspiration that is not *material*.

Believing that both life and community are of great importance, the conservative was forced to reject liberal individualism and socialist collectivism.

As only those with a keen *desire to change society* had the time and energy to conjure economic thinking out of whole cloth, conservatives were left resentful of −and half convinced by− the economic thinking of their opponents.

The question that matters is: why would anyone have a desire to change society?

Burke gives us the answer:

> An ignorant man, who is not fool enough to meddle with this clock, is however sufficiently confident to think he can safely take to pieces, and put together at his pleasure, a moral machine of another guise, importance, and complexity, composed of far other wheels, and springs, and balances and counteracting and co-operating powers.
>
> Their delusive good intention is no sort of excuse for their presumption.

Conservatives have always distrusted economists, because whatever it is they set out to turn people and societies into, it is by definition something they are not, and more often than not something they shouldn't be.

[economists] Whom some regard as the lights of the world and others as incarnate demons, are in general ordinary men, with narrow understandings and little information

THOMAS B. MACAULAY

Chapter 2

Why Economists Cannot Explain What's Going On

By their own admission, economists have often failed to differentiate between their science and their personal-political preferences. Instead of a minute observation of facts and a careful drawing of conclusions that are presented as tentative explanations and never as revealed truth, the public and the decision makers are presented with a host of mutually exclusive "facts" and definitive conclusions that upon observation, prove to be anything but.

Most people are unaware of what any student of statistics knows: Statistics prove absolutely nothing. They merely point the way to potential areas of interest and further study.

Throughout the recent crisis, we watched economists praising initiatives they either knew or ought to have known would not bring about renewed economic vigor and employment (what the public wanted and what politicians claimed to be working toward) but would lead us ever closer to a command economy and therefore to poverty, corruption, stagnation, and social decay.

The public is left with no other option but to trust their own instincts.

Few professions can afford the luxury of twisting and turning reality to suit the personal tastes of their practitioners.

The battle is for the hearts and minds. Economists are, more than any other profession, involved in this battle for liberty, prosperity, and the rule of law versus control, stagnation, and corruption. What is at stake is whether humans are free or *enslaved* by the state, whether there is abundance or scarcity, whether we survive and prosper or sink into terminal decline.

Liberty and humanity have never had many friends among men of learning: humans enjoy life, intellectuals think about it.

Liberty under the law enables those emotional, passionate, creative, and entrepreneurial creatures that go by the name of humankind, to live to the fullest, which is rarely, if ever, the way men of learning would like their inferiors to live.

Friedrich Hayek, a brilliant liberal philosopher and economist, said it in as many words: "We want people to be free to do what *we* want them to do."

The behavior of the economists is not just a matter of intellectual dishonesty. Dishonest, they certainly are, but there is more to it than that.

I do not believe that people can simply be managed. They need to know, or at least to believe, that they are being *led*—and led *somewhere*. That "somewhere" is usually provided by circumstances such as winning a war, resolving a particular issue, or achieving a particular goal.

In times of peace and in the absence of natural disasters, thinkers and intellectuals provide that somewhere. In the West, that somewhere is the planned, rational, global society, or more precisely, the bureaucratic management of humanity for the purpose of eliminating social differences and ushering in equal living conditions.

In the 1930s, Keynes felt that, in view of the great successes of the planned Nazi and Soviet economies (according to the press, not their victims); he should launch a scathing attack on capitalism and on the very idea of freedom:

> Today we suffer disillusion not because we are poorer but because other values seem to have been sacrificed and sacrificed unnecessarily. For our economic system is not, in fact, enabling us to exploit to the utmost the possibilities of our economic wealth afforded by the progress of our technique…leading us to feel we might as well have used up the margin in more satisfying ways.
>
> But once we allow ourselves to be disobedient to the test of an accountant's profit, we have begun to change our civilization.

This is, of course, Karl Marx, speaking with an English accent.

"Having delivered this Ruskinian denunciation of capitalist civilization," Keynes's biographer, Robert Skidelsky, reminds us, "Keynes ended with some words of caution against the silliness of haste and intolerance. But the balance was not well held."

Perhaps defending himself, Keynes later wrote: "Words ought to be a little wild, for they are the assault of thoughts upon the unthinking. But when the seats of power and authority have been attained, there should be no more poetic license." All this was written two years before World War II and the Holocaust.

This is why every economic crisis caused by government meddling in the economy (and they are *all* caused by government meddling) is just another opportunity for more government meddling.

Marx, who described the bureaucratic takeover of the economy he envisaged, told us: "In the beginning this (takeover) cannot be effected except by means of despotic inroads on the rights of property by means of measures which appear economically insufficient and untenable, but which necessitate further inroads upon the old social order."

Does any of this sound like science to you?

With very few exceptions, economists would either prefer a planned economy or believe it to be inevitable. They simply have no time to peddle an alternative and risk their academic careers, their reputations, their government jobs or the chance of a Nobel Prize.

The question is of course: is there anything wrong with a total worldwide bureaucracy or a worldwide *state*?

Surely freedoms will be lost, but the benefits would far outweigh the costs. Sadly, this is not true.

When young girls from developing countries are lured into a life of horror and despair in a Western brothel, they are never told, "Come over here and become a slave," or "We guarantee a horrific life and a brutal death," or "We'll inject you with heroin until you're of no use to us, and then we'll dispose of your wretched body." No, they are lured with promises of a *better* life.

At the start of a nationalized education system, things seem to be going right. But once the last generation of free-thinking teachers is gone, the nationalized system becomes a poverty trap, designed to ensure that only those who can pay get an education. And there is no means of escaping poverty and ignorance for those who cannot.

At the start of a nationalized health care system, things seem to be going right. But once the last generation of free doctors, nurses, and health practitioners is gone, the health care professional becomes a civil servant who has to do as he is told by policymakers. The patients, in turn, have no power of any sort, nowhere else to go, and no idea that things could be any different.

At the start of a national housing policy, things seem to be going right. Workers obtain better housing than they could have ever imagined. Then politicians decide that housing should not be allocated on merit but on "need" (that is, political convenience). Housing projects become dumping grounds for everyone with issues, and the workers see their children dragged into a life of crime, with no hope of employment or betterment of any sort. This never would have happened had they stayed in their working-class neighborhood, where a strong work ethic and sense of community prevailed.

At the start of an environmental policy, things seem to be going right. Then a committed environmentalist is put in charge, and she launches an unrelenting attack on industry and commerce. Companies are made uncompetitive, and millions of jobs are lost (and with them any chance of a decent life for workers and their families). Of course, politicians blame capitalism.

Planned economies don't work unless the *only* purpose of such planning is the well-being (well-being, not equality) of the people. In other words, the planned economy is designed to achieve what a free economy would achieve on its own, only faster.

But even in this best-case scenario, once such well-being has been achieved—if it is ever achieved—planners have nowhere to go. People do not learn to be free just because they are prosperous, particularly if they have learned from an early age that the cause of their prosperity is their very lack of freedom.

Unfree people won't remain prosperous for long. Only a free people can produce a self-sustained civilization and economy, and we —the handful of countries which can be called free— are the first such people in over two millennia.

People are a lot more than a mere collection of needs. But once their liberty and their ability and desire to exercise it are gone, even those needs will go unsatisfied. A slave who is not content with whatever the master gives him will be shown his place. This was true in the Caribbean plantations of the eighteenth century, and it will be true in Europe and America in the twenty-second century if we do not mend our ways.

Adam Smith told us:

> Economists disturb nature in the course of her operations in human affairs; and it requires no more than to let her alone, and give her fair play in the pursuit of her ends that she may establish her own designs.
>
> Little else is requisite to carry a state to the highest degree of opulence from the lowest barbarism, but *peace, easy taxes, and a tolerable administration of justice*; all the rest being brought about by the natural course of things.

A free economy and a free people deeply appreciative of their legacy of liberty are the only antidote against these well-intentioned but ultimately ruinous designs.

Economists know this, and they don't like it one bit.

Starting from the premise of absolute value and dignity of human personality, liberals necessarily demanded freedom for each individual, from the state and from every arbitrary will.

Their sentimental individualism soon became shocked at its own practical consequences: the economic competition and the spiritual isolation which resulted from the triumph of their ideas provoked among them a reaction in favor of powerful benevolent government exercising compulsions.

The "progress" from Jefferson to Roosevelt suggests the rule.
RUSSELL KIRK

CHAPTER 3

WHY FREE MARKETS DISAPPOINT

What do you wish for when you already are the wealthiest, most powerful, most technologically advanced, most educated, best housed, best clothed, best fed, and most productive nation on earth? Change, of course. But not any change: *change you can believe in.*

It would be easy to dismiss the plight of the United States (and most of the developed world, for that matter) as the rich man's blues. It would be easy but it would also be wrong.

There is something much deeper going on. In the past four decades, America has gone from being the place where common folk could enjoy a lifestyle the rest of the world could only envy to a place where workers (and taxpayers) seem to be getting a raw deal. It is difficult to pinpoint exactly what has been lost. Perhaps the hope and excitement of being and doing.

Class warfare is a lot more fun when employers stay, fight, lose, and pay up than when they close up shop and move across the border. Or just close up shop altogether.

For the first two hundred years, the American grassroots experience (and for the past fifty the European experience) was one of movement: farmers' children moving to town, immigrants moving from poverty back home to a land with a future, children of the working classes attaining middle-class status, and middle-class folk moving further up the ladder.

That system was dealt several blows in relatively quick succession, including the establishment of the welfare state, minimum wage legislation; steep, graduated income taxes; the effective ban on immigration; and an education system designed to provide an engaging experience instead of an educational one. And these are just a few.

But the most important blow has been the substantial disappearance of well-paid (and abundant) blue-collar jobs.

Making extraordinary efforts to achieve as much as or possibly a bit less than what your parents and grandparents achieved is hardly inspiring, and it feels like failure. Just as it had happened in Britain a century earlier, mere stability feels like retrogression for a population accustomed to continued material improvement.

What does all of this have to do with free markets and their disappointing nature? The problem is that freedom cuts both ways. Just as businesspeople are free to pursue their business, so are workers. Sadly, while the former usually know what they are doing, the latter are largely at the mercy of the professional politician turned trade union leader.

The disappearance or rather the scarcity of well-paid blue-collar jobs is probably the most damaging of all recent phenomena. The reasons for that loss are many, but they boil down to this: starting at the turn of the twentieth century and accelerating after World War II, those politicians whose political views were too extreme for mainstream politics made their way into the so-called "labor movement."

They figured that if capitalism was the enemy, they should do their bit to *wrestle by degrees all capital from the capitalists* (as Marx had suggested) by making increasingly outlandish demands.

Something had to give, so first the working class was priced out of the market and then large segments of the middle class had their wings clipped, as there was no one to manage.

Together with their friends in mainstream politics, media and education; these leaders convinced workers and the majority of the general public that:

- High taxes were necessary to make the rich pay their fair share, thus taxing for taxing sake; this has depleted the capital stock and severely impaired new capital formation and incentives.

- Strict regulations were necessary to ensure quality and environmental standards. This made it impossible for new competitors to enter any market and hire workers, which led to higher unemployment and lower real wages.
- Extravagant pension and health care arrangements were necessary, and they would not impact the viability of companies. This guaranteed the bankruptcy of all, or substantially all, heavy industry in Britain and America.
- It was necessary for the government to establish high minimum wages to protect vulnerable workers. Thus pricing underprivileged groups out of the market, condemning them to a life on welfare.
- It was necessary for government workers to retire as early as possible to make space for new workers. Thus it condemned generations to exorbitant taxation and lousy public services, while creating a captive electoral clientele.
- It was necessary that legal immigration should be curtailed to protect jobs. This deprived the country of fresh ideas, talents, and enthusiasm and created the blot of tens of millions of illegal immigrants.
- It was necessary that the state have a monopoly on education. This killed any hope of true political and ideological diversity and the healthy debate and flurry of ideas they foster. If we are all progressive, there is no possibility of true progress.
- It was necessary that the state have a monopoly on health care. This increased bureaucracy and cost, and reduced innovation.
- It was necessary that the state have a monopoly in the provision for unemployment and old age, thereby setting up the country for moral and financial bankruptcy.

The freedom to choose includes the freedom to choose what's bad for us.

The results of those policies are there for all to see:

- Companies and individuals desperately try to shelter what they have from taxation (and inflation) when they should be spending their time and talents creating wealth and jobs.
- Foreign manufacturers replace domestic ones due to extreme environmental regulation and taxation at home.

- Nations go bust, "resentful yet mendicant like, fearful of consolidation but cursed with an insatiable appetite for grants-in-aid."
- The banking system goes bankrupt.
- The currency is debased.
- Generations are wasted and lives destroyed, along with hopes, families, and communities.
- Misery, frustration, violence, and repression become apparent.
- Liberties and constitutional privileges are suppressed.
- A permanent underclass develops.
- In the world of ideas, there is no discernible diversity.

After exploring the United States back in the 1840s, liberal social scientist and thinker Alexis de Tocqueville warned us,

> I think, then, that the species of oppression by which democratic nations are menaced is unlike anything that ever before existed in the world; our contemporaries will find no prototype of it in their memories.
>
> I seek in vain for an expression that will accurately convey the whole idea I have formed of it; the old words despotism and tyranny are inappropriate; the thing itself is new and since I cannot name it, I must attempt to define it.
>
> The first thing that strikes the observation is an innumerable multitude of men, all equal and all alike.
>
> Each of them, living apart, is as a stranger to the fate of all the rest; his children and his private friends constitute to him the whole of mankind.
>
> As for the rest of his fellow citizens he is close to them but he does not see them, he touches them, but he does not feel them, he exists only in himself and for himself alone, and if his kindred still remain to him, he may be said at any rate to have lost his country. Above this race of men stands an immense and tutelary power, which takes upon itself alone to secure their gratifications and to watch over their fate.
>
> That power is absolute, minute, regular, provident, and mild.
>
> It would be like the authority of a parent if, like that authority, its object was to prepare men for manhood; but it seeks, on the contrary, to keep them in perpetual childhood.

For their happiness such a government willingly labors but it chooses to be the only arbiter of their necessities, facilitates their pleasures, manages their principal concerns, directs their industry, regulates the descent of property, and subdivides their inheritances; what remains but to spare them all the care of thinking and all the trouble of living?

Thus every day renders the exercise of the free agency of man less useful and less frequent; it circumscribes the will within a narrower range and gradually robs a man of all the uses of himself, the principle of equality has prepared men for these things; it has predisposed them to endure them and often to look on them as benefits.

A century later, in the 1940s, Kirk commented;

Here a kind of humanitarian Egyptian or Peruvian society is described, just the sort of state British and American collectivistic reformers project today.

Most advocates of the planned economy, indeed, hardly are able to understand Tocqueville's loathing for an existence like this.

The omnicompetent, paternalistic state, guiding all the affairs of mankind, satisfying all individuals' wants, is the ideal of the twentieth century planner.

This arrangement is intended to gratify the material demands of humanity, and twentieth century social aspirations, so saturated with the ideas of Bentham and Marx, scarcely conceive of wants that are not material.

That men be kept in perpetual childhood—that in spirit they never become full human beings—seems no great a loss to a generation of thinkers accustomed to compulsory schooling, compulsory insurance, compulsory military service, and even compulsory voting.

It's the economy, stupid!

Whether you believe the world described above to be heaven on earth (if you are a liberal) or a "veritable Hell of Civilization" (if you are not) is less relevant than this simple fact of life: all those individuals who hope for an "omnicompetent, paternalistic state, guiding all the affairs of mankind, satisfying all individuals' wants" assume the *economics of plenty*. In other words, they assume that productive economic activity will continue undeterred regardless of the level of regulation and taxation. This assumption is unfounded. The overbearing tax and regulatory framework hinders economic activity forcing the government to "rescue" those industries it unwittingly set out to destroy

Then the blame is apportioned on those who have still managed to make a life for themselves, despite all the government intervention: the privileged, the rich, the capitalists, the top 1 percent.

Then there are more taxes, more bureaucrats, more politicians, more regulation, and more redistribution of a shrinking pie.

As Ronald Reagan so eloquently put it:

> Government's view on the economy could be summed up in a
> few short phrases: if it moves, tax it. If it keeps moving, regu-
> late it. If it stops moving, subsidize it.

Think about this for a moment: the state, government, professional politicians, and bureaucrats all have existed since the dawn of civilization. *General prosperity* and *genuine social progress*, on the other hand, have existed only for a few decades in a few countries. Those few decades and those few countries where the state, government, professional politicians, and bureaucrats were restrained, they were restrained either by visionary members of their own class or by a popular mistrust of government interference. You draw your own conclusions.

What has never worked is presented as the solution, yet the only thing that works is presented as the problem.

To claim that governments can "help the economy" is the economic equivalent of claiming that machines can create energy. It has never happened, it will never happen, and by the second law of thermodynamics, it cannot happen.

Free markets do not disappoint people who are happy to be free and to take their profits when they get it right and to endure their losses when they get it wrong. Those people, however, are few and far between and become fewer and farther between with every new generation that is educated to expect everything from society.

In a democracy it pays to pander to people's desires without criticizing them. The result is almost invariably a loss of freedom and prosperity. If people cannot control their cravings, we put a ban on advertising certain food. If people become disorderly, we claim that the people have a right to be angry.

In more practical matters, certain people choose to take business risks in areas with few prospects and then complain that the government does not give them enough money. Individuals train in particular fields of their liking with little regard for their own subsequent employability and then complain that the government does not invest enough money in that field. Someone chooses job security and then feels shocked when a former colleague, who took risks, does well for herself. Conversely, someone who chooses to take chances in life and fails is horrified to find out that those who did not risk much are doing better than they are.

We are disappointed with freedom because
we are never free to have our cake and eat it too.

In the public's defense I can confidently say this: every program, every tax, every privilege, every piece of legislation designed to deter wealth and job creation and to put an end to liberty and prosperity has been sold as necessary, beneficial and fair by politicians and economists alike. They are of course free to say whatever they want even if it isn't true.

Economists of great fame and acclaim have defended free markets in their own peculiar ways.

Next we cover the two thinkers I consider pivotal in the development of the free economy, which was a feature of life in the 1714–1914 period, particularly in Britain and her dominions. These free-market apologists are Adam Smith and David Ricardo.

ADAM SMITH (1723-1790)

A moralist, professor of moral philosophy, Lord Rector of Glasgow University.[4*]

Aptly called the father of modern economics, of the four most influential economists covered in detail in this essay, Adam Smith is the only one to employ the method of observation, and thence the only one whose writings can be honestly defined as "scientific" in any sense of the word.

Smith was "a man of the Enlightenment," or more precisely, a man of the Scottish Enlightenment.

The Scottish Enlightenment is fundamentally different from its Continental counterpart in that it aimed at finding answers by observation of phenomena. The Continental Enlightenment follows on the rationalistic tradition of apriorism (just like Ricardo, Marx, and Keynes, the other three economists covered in this text).

[4*] All the extracts that follow are from *An Inquiry into the Nature and Causes of the Wealth of Nations* (New York: Penguin Classics, 1986), which first appeared in 1776.

Apriorism can be summed up as follows: this is what I and my friends believe. Since we cannot possibly be wrong, it must be true.

This is why conservatives can draw valuable input from the thinkers of the Scottish Enlightenment and hardly anything of value from their Continental counterparts.

Ricardo, Marx, and Keynes never burdened themselves with observation. They first elaborated on their conclusions by supporting or denouncing Smith or the classical economists in general and then proceeded to find the "incontrovertible proof," either logical or factual, that they were right.

Strict but ultimately unsound logic and a new lexicon prevailed in the case of Ricardo. Carefully selected "facts" prevailed in the case of Marx. The rephrasing of Marx —to suit contemporary audiences— prevailed in the case of Keynes.

Modern economists are fond of disparaging Smith as an anachronism. Smith is, however, the last influential *man of ideas* to approach economics as a scientist. His observations are as valid today as they were over two centuries ago and just as useful.

I will use a two pronged approach to this most influential work:

1. What we should learn from Adam Smith.
2. Where he went wrong. As a moralist, Smith does not always appeals to observation. There are deeply un-conservative statements in his writings. His value to us comes from the acuity and honesty of his economic and political observations, not from his moral philosophy.)

The world is not and was not what Smith had in mind. The world was full of unproductive people—namely, "priests, teachers, thinkers, physicians, politicians, civil servants, soldiers, the aristocracy, writers, actors, and singers." His world would have resembled an ant colony or a beehive; only he would have also done away with the queen and the soldiers as idle and unnecessary.

All worker bees and ants, enjoying the fruits of their labors until they are all dead.

In Smith we begin to observe the poisonous streak, which would pave the way for the spiritual desert of the twentieth century.

A Smithian world would be totally devoid of beauty—other than beautiful machinery—and would serve no other purpose than the propagation of efficient human material, in other words a world not worth conserving.

The conservative policymaker relies on Smith and his successors, not because she agrees with the beehive philosophy of man, but on the contrary, because the more efficient we become at producing what we want, the more time we have *to be truly human*; that is to create and to enjoy all that beauty and merriment Smith would have rather done without.

By making possible or greatly facilitating the existence and the survival of liberty, prosperity and the rule of law, the free market is the means, not the end of conservative policymaking.

From Smith we learn:

1. That the incredibly advanced state of our society and economy was not the result of deliberate government action:

   "The greatest improvement in the productive powers of labor, and the greater part of the skill, dexterity, and judgment with which it is anywhere directed, or applied, seem to have been the effects of the division of labor" (109).

   "this division of labor, from which so many advantages are derived, is not originally the effect of any human wisdom" (117).

2. That the public needs to always be alert to and wary of the combination of special interests. This was true in his day of both workers and employers, just as it is true today of professional politicians, community activists, non-viable industries, and everyone who wants a special advantage at everybody else's expense:

   "People of the same trade seldom meet together, even for merriment and diversion, but the conversation ends in a conspiracy against the public" (232).

3. That there is something *fundamentally immoral* every time the governments take too much of someone's income (God demanded 10 percent, politicians everywhere demand 40, 50, 60 percent and have been known to demand more than 90 percent):

   "The property which every man has in his own labor, as it is the original foundation of all other property, so it is the most sacred and inviolable." (225)

4. That few have, and even fewer will, risk ruin for the vague probability of improvement in their fellow humans' living conditions unless he can convince his financial investors that there is the chance of unusually high

rewards (which on a risk-adjusted basis turn out to be not that unusually high):

"The establishment of any new manufacture, or any new branch of commerce, or of any new practice in agriculture, is always speculation, from which the projector promises himself extraordinary profits" (218).

5. That creditworthy people and countries get richer infinitely faster than would otherwise be the case by the mere fact that people with money will lend to them abundantly and cheaply, enabling them to undertake improvements which would have taken much longer had their reputation been poorer:

"The credit of a frugal and thriving man increases much faster than his stock. His trade is extended in proportion to the amount of both and the sum or amount of his profits is in proportion to the extent of his trade and his annual accumulation in proportion to the amount of his profits" (216).

6. That the wealthier a country becomes, the number of the idle, both rich and poor, will diminish (increasing wealth even further as a result):

"In a country which had acquired its full complement of riches the rate of interest [will be] so low as to render it impossible for any but the very wealthiest people to live upon the interest of their money" (199).

7. That contrary to popular belief, it is the poor who are to benefit the most from a strict enforcement of contracts:

"When the law does not enforce the performance of contracts, it puts all borrowers nearly upon the same footing with bankrupts or people of doubtful credit in better regulated countries" (198).

8. That the only solution to bad, stingy employers, is more bad, stingy employers competing with each other for the services of labor (also true of excessive profits and also that Ricardo, and through him, Marx got the nature of capital accumulations and wages upside down as we'll see later on):

"As riches, improvement and population have increased, interest (and the profits of capital) has declined. The wages of labor do not sink with the profits of stock.

"The demand for labor increases with the increase of stock whatever be its profits; and after these are diminished, stock may not only continue to increase, but to increase much faster than before. A great stock, though with small profits, generally increases faster than a small stock with great profits." (195)

"The increase of stock, which raises wages, tends to lower profit." (190)

9. That (Keynes notwithstanding) the wealthier the members of a society become the wealthier that society and by extension all societies become:
"As the capital of a private man may increase beyond what he can employ so likewise the capital of a great nation" (194).

10. That unless it is deliberately interrupted, the process of wealth creation tends to be self-sustained and self-reinforced, and that a growing economy is the best news for workers:
"In years of plenty, servants frequently leave their masters, and trust their subsistence to what they can make by their own industry" (186).

From a purely political standpoint, that is relating to the actual management of the state, we learn:

1. That "no society can surely be flourishing and happy of which the far greater part of the members are poor and miserable. It is but equity besides that they who feed, clothe, and lodge the whole body of the people should have such a share of the produce of their own labor as to be themselves tolerably well fed, clothed, and lodged" (181).

2. That "in a country where the funds destined for the maintenance of labor were sensibly decaying every year the demand for laborers would in all the different classes of employments be less than it had been the year before. Many, who had been bred in the superior classes not being able to find employment in their own business, would be glad to seek it in the lowest" (175).

3. That while investors will only invest and employ people when it makes sense to do it, people will have children whenever they want to. *No country is ever too rich* to be able to discourage investment (or to redistribute the funds destined thereto) without risking unemployment or underemployment and the consequent poverty and misery:
"The demand for those who live by wages necessarily increases with the increase of the revenue and stock of every country and *cannot possibly increase without it*. The increase of revenue and stock is the increase of national wealth.

The demand for those who live by wages, therefore, naturally increases with the increase of national wealth, and *cannot possibly increase without it.*

It is not the actual greatness of national wealth, but its *continual increase,* which occasions a rise in the wages of labor." (172)

4. That the best way to generate "business confidence" is for the government to do what it claims it would do, and to refrain from doing what it promised not to do. Once this is cleared there is no reason to believe that investment would not be forthcoming:

   "In all countries where there is tolerable security, every man of common understanding will endeavor to employ whatever stock he can command in procuring either present enjoyment or future profit. In those unfortunate countries, where men are continually afraid of the violence of their superiors, they frequently bury and conceal a great part of their stock, in order to have it always at hand to carry with them to some place of safety."(380)

Looking at the risks taken by people to take their money out of our countries, one wonders if Europe, America, and Japan should be added to the list of "unfortunate countries" where men are continually afraid of the violence of their superiors. In Smith's time the list included Turkey, India, and most of Asia. Perhaps it is time to expand the list.

5. That to improve the lot of the worker, the best thing is to ensure that savings and investments are never discouraged, either by taxation or by spending policies:

   "The intention of the fixed capital is to increase the productive powers of labor or to enable the same number of laborers to perform a much greater quantity of work." (383)

6. That before capitalism gave us the modern world, for thousands of years; there were brutal governments, which gave us war, torture, rape, famine, and slavery.

   "Commerce and manufactures gradually introduced order and good government, and with them, the liberty and security of the individuals, among the inhabitants of the country, who had before lived, almost in a continual state of war with their neighbors and of servile dependency upon their superiors." (508)

7. That a penny in the hands of those who earned it is worth a thousand in the hands of a politician or civil servant:
   "A merchant is accustomed to employ his money chiefly in profitable projects, whereas a country gentleman is accustomed to employ it chiefly in expense" (507)

8. That if men are not allowed to enjoy the fruits of their labors and retain them after taxes, they will make no efforts and/or will pay no taxes:
   "Men in a defenseless state naturally content themselves with their necessary subsistence, because to acquire more might only tempt the injustice of their oppressors.
   On the contrary, when they are secure of enjoying the fruits of their industry, they naturally exert it to better their condition and to acquire not only the necessaries but the conveniences and elegances of life." (502)

9. A warning against regulatory and legislative enthusiasm:
   "Laws frequently continue in force long after the circumstances which first gave occasion to them and which could alone render them reasonable, are no more." (485)

Finally, a word of warning to all those individuals who believe that everyone in society should become a full-time philanthropist whether he wants to or not: the best program for social advancement ever created is called 'a job.'

> As every individual, therefore, endeavors as much as he can both to employ his capital in the support of domestic industry, and so to direct that industry that its produce may be of the greatest value; every individual necessarily labors to render the annual revenue of the society as great as he can.
> He generally, indeed, neither intends to promote the public interest, nor knows how much he is promoting it.
> By preferring the support of domestic to that of foreign industry, he intends only his own security; and by directing that industry in such a manner as its produce may be of the greatest value, he intends only his own gain, and he is in this, as in many other cases, led by an invisible hand to promote an end which was no part of his intention.
> Nor is it always the worse for the society that it was no part of it. By pursuing his own interest he frequently promotes that of the society more effectually than when he really intends to promote it.

WHERE DID SMITH GO WRONG?

Where Smith gets it all wrong, unfortunately, is in his understanding of men's behavior and motives:

> This division of labor, from which so many advantages are derived, is not originally the effect of any human wisdom, which foresees and intends that general opulence to which it gives occasion. It is the necessary, though very slow and gradual, consequence of a certain propensity in human nature which has in view no such extensive utility; the propensity to truck, barter, and exchange one thing for another.
>
> Whether this propensity be one of those original principles in human nature, of which no further account can be given; or whether, as seems more probable, it be the necessary consequence of the faculties of reason and speech, it belongs not to our present subject to enquire. It is common to all men, and to be found in no other race of animals, which seem to know neither this nor any other species of contracts.
>
> Two greyhounds, in running down the same hare, have sometimes the appearance of acting in some sort of concert. Each turns her towards his companion, or endeavors to intercept her when his companion turns her towards himself. This, however, is not the effect of any contract, but of the accidental concurrence of their passions in the same object at that particular time. Nobody ever saw a dog make a fair and deliberate exchange of one bone for another with another dog.

The statements above can only be described as astonishing. Greyhounds, like all other kinds of animals that hunt in a pack (including humans), are organized in hierarchical, pyramid-like structures. They all hunt together and *act in concert*, but when it comes to sharing the booty, those at the top of the pyramid eat first and those at the bottom eat last. Simple. If there is enough, fine, if there isn't enough those at the bottom (or more likely, their offspring) simply starve to death, regardless of the effort they have applied to the hunting enterprise.

Humans have behaved in the same fashion for most of our history. In the case of a nuclear holocaust today, all the top politicians of the developed world would be saved, but very few civilians and then only those who are considered of particular importance or usefulness.

Accounts of medieval kings who feasted while the *court* went hungry are another example.

All animal societies and most human societies are organized by status (birth, brute force, or both). It is the slow, partial, imperfect transition from *status to contract, from the social arrangements we had in common with dogs and hyenas to a social arrangement which could only exist in a human society, that* we can with any degree of accuracy call "social progress."

But this statement is remarkable for another reason. Professor Smith was based in Glasgow, a great commercial center at the time. It was plain for all to see that the underlying source of the city's wealth was ownership or at least access to the produce of the Caribbean plantations, whose land had been acquired by force, and whose workforce had been brutally enslaved. This should have been obvious to the professor, unless he considered the stolen land and the forcefully enslaved workforce as just another manifestation of the "pretty machinery" he describes in the preceding chapter.
"[There is] certain propensity in human nature...; the propensity to truck, barter, and exchange one thing for another" or the human propensity to steal, to kill, and to enslave? In other words, the human propensity is to see other humans as the means to an end.

But then the killer blow comes along, almost unexpectedly:

> The difference of natural talents in different men is, in reality, much less than we are aware of; and the very different genius which appears to distinguish men of different professions, when grown up to maturity, is not upon many occasions so much the cause, as the effect of the division of labor.
> The difference between the most dissimilar characters, between a philosopher and a common street porter, for example, seems to arise not so much from nature, as from habit, custom, and education.
> When they came into the world, and for the first six or eight years of their existence, they were perhaps, very much alike, and neither their parents nor playfellows could perceive any remarkable difference.

Smith's biographer tells us that "this statement is apparently directed against Harris' *Money and Coins*, and is in accordance with the view of Hume, who asks readers to "consider how nearly equal all men are in their bodily force, and even in their mental powers and faculties, where cultivated by education."

The astonishing Marxist and Keynesian claims that the entrepreneur *could and should* be replaced by a clerk stem directly from this absurd conjectures.

These conjectures are, of course, an extension of John Locke's belief in "tabula rasa" and "environmental conditioning" to the field of economics and have done more damage to the economies of the world than the most exploitative forms of taxation could have ever achieved.

It never crossed Hume's or Smith's mind that the differences in industry, talent and ambition, desire, determination, discipline, and dedication between men could be of a *fundamental* nature and that education may only play as a secondary although important role in maximizing or minimizing the ability and desire to put that industry, talent, and ambition to good use.

Three horror stories come out of this confusion:

1. The appalling abuse and mistreatment of the poor in nineteenth-century Britain, at Malthus' behest (If Hume and Smith were right all "the poor" needed was to be taught the right "habits, customs, and education," despite the fact that elsewhere in his writings Smith rejects the idea of providing this "education" at government expense. Lest those so educated compete on equal terms with those who actually paid for the privilege out of their own pockets.)
2. The nationalization of the "means of production, distribution, and exchange" advocated by Marx and effected —to varying degrees— in the twentieth century. Why should we tolerate businesspeople making money when they can be easily replaced by low-paid clerks who've been provided the right "habit, custom, and education."
3. Keynes's contention is the government official and not the "ignorant" entrepreneur should direct investment, and again, the government and not individuals who should direct spending.

It would not be too far off the mark to say that this single statement, grounded more on romantic ideas of natural equality than in actual observation, has caused more economic destruction than the most eccentric fabrications of Marx and Keynes.

He keeps getting it wrong:

> The absurd opinion that riches consist in money had given rise to "many prejudicial errors in practice," such as the prohibition of the exportation

of coin and attempts to secure a favorable balance of trade. There will always be plenty of money if things are left to their free course, and no prohibition of exportation will be effectual. The desire to secure a favorable balance of trade has led to 'most pernicious regulations' such as the restrictions on trade with France.

This is most certainly true when the vast majority of the population is attached to the land and largely debt free. A sudden collapse in the money supply would reduce the amount of goods the people can buy, but these represented a small fraction of their total basket. In a world exhibiting vast urban populations, heavily indebted and entirely dependent on wages for their subsistence, a sudden collapse in the money supply would lead to a level of penury simply unimaginable in Smith's time.

Admittedly, substantial urban populations were only beginning to emerge at the time of Smith's writings.

SMITH AS POLITICAL ACTIVIST AND PAMPHLETEER

Agriculture was hindered by great tracts of land being thrown into the hands of single persons.

This led at first to cultivation by slaves, who had no motive to industry; then came tenants by steel bow who had no sufficient inducement to improve the land; finally the present method of cultivation by tenants was introduced, but these for a long time were insecure in their holdings, and had to pay rent in kind, which made them liable to be severely affected by bad seasons.

Feudal subsidies discouraged industry, the law of primogeniture, entails, and the expense of transferring land prevented the large estates from being divided.

The restrictions on the export of corn helped to stop the progress of agriculture.

Progress in arts and commerce was also hindered by slavery, as well as by the ancient contempt for industry and commerce, by the want of enforcement of contracts, by the various difficulties and dangers of transport, by the establishment of fairs, markets and staple towns, by duties on imports and exports, and by monopolies, corporation privileges, the statute of apprenticeship and bounties (subsidies).

Here, Smith jumps straight into the class struggle taking place between the self-made men, and the established landed interests of late eighteenth-century Britain, on the side of the self-made Glasgow men.

He may just as well have said: end private ownership of land and the right of inheritance, because in any case, my patrons already have their fortunes safely tucked away.

An outline of the theory of alienation later popularized by Marx:

> But certain inconveniences arise from a commercial spirit. Men's views are confined, and when a person's whole attention is bestowed on the seventeenth part of a pin or the eightieth part of a button, he becomes stupid.
>
> Education is neglected. In Scotland the meanest porter can read and write, but at Birmingham boys of six or seven can earn three-pence or sixpence a day, so that their parents set them to work early and their education is neglected.
>
> To be able merely to read is good as it gives people the benefit of religion, which is a great advantage, not only considered in a pious sense, but as it affords them subject for thought and speculation.
>
> There is too another great loss which attends the putting boys too soon to work. The boys throw off parental authority, and betake themselves to drunkenness and riot.
>
> The workmen in the commercial parts of England are consequently in a despicable condition; their work through half the week is sufficient to maintain them, and through want of education they have no amusement for the other but riot and debauchery.
>
> So it may very justly be said that the people who clothe the whole world are in rags themselves.

This passage can be described as a collection of platitudes. In any case to list the absurdities in this lamentable paragraph is tiresome and dismaying, but it has to be done.

- A highly specialized worker "becomes stupid." Smith was himself a highly specialized worker.
- As he "becomes stupid" education is neglected. This ignores that he may have chosen to educate himself to pursue such specialization (doctors, lawyers,

teachers, bricklayers, etc.), or that he may have landed the job, because he had not received much in the form of an education. It never follows that having become specialized, he *subsequently* neglects his education.

- The Scottish poor can read and write, but this does not improve their material condition.
- Six-year–old, illiterate English boys earn more than a literate adult in Scotland. If this were true, they would have moved.
- Parents who send their children to work have ample resources to educate them if they so choose (all those programs to end "child factory labor" in the Third World, which condemn lower income children to prostitution and crime, stem from this confusion).
- Boys sent to work "throw off parental authority." How? By giving their parents every penny they earn as it was and is customary?
- Boys working twelve-hour days seven days a week have time to riot.

We owe so much to this man that we have to finish this section on a high note.

From certain lectures professor Smith gave at Edinburgh in the winter of 1750–1751 a few statements of outstanding –almost prophetic– acuity, reach us:

> Man is generally considered by economists as the materials of a sort of political mechanics.
>
> Economists disturb nature in the course of her operations in human affairs; and it requires no more than to let her alone, and give her fair play in the pursuit of her ends that she may establish her own designs.
>
> Little else is requisite to carry a state to the highest degree of opulence from the lowest barbarism, but peace, easy taxes, and a tolerable administration of justice; all the rest being brought about by the natural course of things.
>
> All governments which thwart this natural course, which force things into another channel (like Keynes) or which endeavor to arrest the progress of society at a particular point (like Marx), are unnatural and to support themselves are obliged to be oppressive and tyrannical.

Written in 1750, this last paragraph can only be described as prophetic.

David Ricardo (1772–1823)

Note: Ricardo is important to those attempting to understand economics, because his influence has been enormous and is still with us today, either directly or through Karl Marx's writings.

Just like Marx, Ricardo got everything wrong in the field of economics, and his misconceptions lie at the root of many of our most destructive policies.

Learning what he said and why is, I hope, the first step towards understanding what we are doing wrong and what we should do instead.

Leaving high school at the age of fourteen, Ricardo followed in his father's footsteps in the London Stock Exchange, where he made a considerable fortune. He became interested in economics after reading Adam Smith's *The Wealth of Nations* in 1799 on a vacation to the English resort of Bath.

This was Ricardo's first contact with economics. He wrote his first economics article at age thirty-seven, and within another ten years he had reached the height of his fame. His ideas had a tremendous influence on later developments in economics, particularly in the area of international trade. He condenses his ideas in his most important work, *Principles of Political Economy and Taxation*, which first appeared in 1816.

In the social and political arena, his misconceptions in the area of wages and profits may have prompted Karl Marx to develop his ideas on class warfare. (Ricardo paints the relationship between employers and employees as *fundamentally* inimical and irreconcilable since [according to Ricardo's interpretation] the wages of the latter can *only* ever originate from a loss of profits of the former, while the profits of the former can only stem from the starvation of the latter.)

As usual, the most influential economists aren't economists at all but keen enthusiasts unhindered by observation, common sense, any sense of historical or social responsibility, or in this case, formal education.

In the case of Ricardo, Joseph Schumpeter coined the term "Ricardian vice," which indicates that rigorous logic does not provide a good economic theory, a criticism that now applies to most economic theories that make heavy use of mathematics to arrive at unsound conclusions.

A good argument is not necessarily a good policy.

Ricardo's writings gave rise to a number of early socialists in the 1820s, who argued that his value theory (the so-called "labor theory of value") had radical implications.

They argued that, in view of the labor theory of value, labor produces the entire product, and the profits capitalists get are a result of the exploitation of workers. Needless to say, this tragic misunderstanding (the labor theory of value, which has a lot more to do with misguided humanism, even social primitivism, than with economics), is still with us today and lies at the base of all economic mismanagement and the lunatic theories of political economy that have cost millions of lives and *may still prove the final undoing of Western civilization.*

Before we move on, we need to define a few concepts that, I believe, are worth committing to memory, as they are the cornerstone of all understanding in the field of economics: the concept of value and the concept of price.

Value, which is anything that one seeks to acquire or preserve, is a subjective measure. No two human beings value the same things in the same way: In other words, one man's trash is another man's treasure. Price, on the other hand, is the amount as of money or goods, asked for or given in exchange for something else.

It should be obvious that at one point or another, the rubber meets the road—that is, at some point acquiring or preserving (disposing or relinquishing) something can and will mean giving something up or accepting something in exchange.

Value and price become somehow connected. There is a salary that gets a man out of bed, and one that doesn't. There is a price at which I buy that car, and a price at which I don't. Matching value and price is difficult at the best of times.

But because every person's valuation of his own time and even of his own life is different from that of the next person, it is simply not possible to have an absolute, invariable, and universally acceptable measure of value of any kind.

Smith told us, and Ricardo echoed, that labor alone never varying in its own value, is alone the ultimate and real standard by which the value of all commodities can at all times and places be estimated and compared. Ricardo actually rephrased this statement as "it is the comparative quantity of commodities which labor will produce that determines their present or past relative value, and not the comparative quantities of commodities which are given to the laborer in exchange for his labor."

The use of the word *relative* implies that people's only motivation is envy, something patently false, since many are also motivated by lust, greed, gluttony, sloth, wrath, and pride.

The assumptions one would have to concede to make the above even plausible are so farfetched that one starts to wonder what on earth these people were thinking (that by *labor* we mean the food necessary to maintain the laborer for the duration of the job; that organizing, financing, insuring, supervising, designing, advertising, commercializing, and the overall management, protection, and preservation of the state, and so on happen all by themselves and are worthless and costless, to name but a few)

One is almost tempted to suggest that if labor is the standard of all value—and by *labor* we mean the bare subsistence of the laborer—we may be dealing with the value system of Mother Nature. To build this house cost Mother Nature fifty pounds of wheat, for example. Or one might suggest we deal with God's value system, since every minute a person is working she is unlikely to be praying and presumably all prayers are of the same value to The Divinity.

But then again we would be talking about the value of a particular entity—divine or otherwise—not the ultimate and real standard of value, which cannot possibly exist.

Granted, Ricardo was a high school dropout. Smith —who was wrong about the labor theory of value, but understood the difference between the value and the price of labor, that is the wage— paints a different picture:

> The demand for labor increases with the increase of stock whatever be its profits; and after these are diminished, stock may not only continue to increase, but to increase much faster than before....A great stock, though with small profits, generally increases faster than a small stock with great profits. (195)

The increase of stock, which *raises* wages, tends to lower profit. (190)
This is what Ricardo (and through him Marx) understood:

> Profits depend on high or low wages, wages on the price of necessaries, and the price of necessaries chiefly on the price of food.

And thus the economic "foundation" for revolutionary upheaval was laid, and three hundred years of evidence to the contrary are not going to change that.

"Audiences are always better pleased with a smart retort, some joke or epigram, than with any amount of reasoning [or evidence, one may add]."

The plot thickens.

At the time of Ricardo's fame, the dominant school of thought was "utilitarianism" or "the greatest happiness of the greatest number."

Since this school, whose leading lights (Jeremy Bentham and James Mill) befriended and heavily influenced Ricardo made no provisions as to any limitation to the pain inflicted to those who were not part of "the greatest number," they were referred to by conservatives as "brutilitarians."

To objectivize what is by definition subjective (value), one needs to create a fictional subject that is in all respects identical (and equipollent) to all other subjects: a subject that is in fact an object. Only by turning the subject into an object, could they render objective what is in fact subjective.

It follows that one should seek the lowest common (observable) denominator among all those subjects. Despite Marx's contention that *capitalists* see people as objects, it is in fact the economist (Marx included) who does just that.

"'Man' is generally considered by economists as the materials of a sort of political mechanics." (Adam Smith)

The lowest common denominator across all humans is our biology (humans are animals, which as such should be scientifically farmed). And, presto, the satisfaction of material needs is the only measure of happiness, and labor (the exertion we can extract after satisfying material needs) is the only invariable measure of value.

Needless to say, if all people are identical, their material needs cannot be different, so nothing but the absolute equality of living conditions, regardless of any other consideration, would satisfy the liberal (now turned socialist) economist.

This leaves us with the definition of "material needs" (and where to get the money to satisfy them, but that's for another chapter), which, granted the assumption that all people are not just equal but identical, can be established from time to time by properly trained economists, maybe with the help of nutritionists and experts in sanitation.

Under this fantastical theoretical framework, designed for a beehive with no queen or soldiers, labor is the "ultimate and real standard of value."

- All people *belong* to the state (the state in turn is entrusted to the economists).
- The state's only purpose is to make the majority of people happy.
- It is up to economists to define what is meant by *happy*.
- Anything other than physical work (thinking, planning, executing, and supervising) is carried out by the officials of the state, who are not in

the business of being happy themselves but of dishing out happiness to others.

- Everything we spend on each worker is a cost to the state.
- Labor (that is, the cost of labor in terms of food) is the ultimate and real standard of value, and value is cost to the state or to Mother Nature or to the universe.

That this line of thinking is fundamentally illiberal is patently obvious. So it is no surprise that, in a few years, someone would put together utilitarianism and Ricardian economics and take them to their ultimate logical conclusion. Such a conclusion would come from an idealist, but let's not anticipate.

The ultimate logical conclusion of this line of thinking is a human farm with intellectuals as planners, bureaucrats (and the security apparatus) as farmers, and the rest of humankind as the farmed, all perfectly compliant with the scientific definition of happy *and* therefore happy. Those who do not comply should be humanely disposed of. Or maybe inhumanely disposed of *pour décourager les autres*. (to be made an example of)

It was only a matter of time before humans who cost so much in terms of natural resources (the ultimate measure of cost by those idealists who believe they own −or have to save− the universe) would come to be seen by intellectuals as parasites whose demise should be actively pursued by all means possible.

If current economic, political, and demographic trends continue, by the end of this century liberalism would have succeeded in exterminating those groups on which it was inflicted—namely, that section of humankind formerly known as Christendom, plus Japan.

Conservatives realized from the very beginning that liberalism was nothing more than a societal death wish. And we should not be surprised that so many ideas produced by the liberal mind would lead sooner or later to our demise.

So, what did Ricardo actually say, and what does it mean for us?

In chapter one of his *Principles of Political Economy and Taxation*, Ricardo had to convince his reader that the laborer is the only entity in the universe that actually *creates value*.

This is the economic equivalent of arguing that it was the quill that wrote Hamlet, not Shakespeare, whose only achievement was to find himself —entirely by chance— *oppressing and exploiting* the quill at the time of writing.

1. "Possessing utility [which he defines as the ability to contribute to human gratification], commodities derive their exchangeable value from two sources: from their scarcity, and from the quantity of labor required to obtain them."

    This seemingly innocent statement spelled the death sentence for hundreds of millions of people the world over (particularly in Russia and her colonies, China, North Korea, and Cambodia)—first, successful farmers, manufacturers, wholesalers, retailers, financiers, and second, the millions of workers whose livelihoods depended on the ability and success of these entrepreneurs. If only the laborer creates value, everyone else is a parasite and should be destroyed or reeducated to become a laborer.

2. "If labor fell very considerably in value and if I found that its fall was in consequence of an abundant supply, encouraged by the great facility with which corn, and the other necessaries of the laborer, were produced, it would, I apprehend, be correct for me to say that corn and necessaries had fallen in value in consequence of less quantity of labor being necessary to produce them, and that this facility of providing for the support of the laborer had been followed by a fall in the value of labor."

- There are so many ifs here that one should probably discard the statement as highly speculative. Ricardo, however, uses it as the basis for everything that follows. Let's have a look: "If labor fell very considerably in value." Value has nothing to do with this; he means price expressed in cash terms—that is, the wage.

- "If I found its fall was in consequence of an abundant supply." An abundant supply of workers will not trigger a diminution in wages unless it is accompanied by a shrinking economy, perfect competition (and fungibility) of workers, and so on. Labor can be abundant and their salaries high at the same time. Or, indeed, scarce and cheap.

- "Encouraged by the great facility with which corn and other necessaries of the laborer, were produced." This is precious: since entrepreneurs and workers are much better at doing what they used to do, it follows that all their spare time and resources would never give occasion to new industries, new products, and new things to do. This is very Aristotelian, but neither Aristotle nor Ricardo knew much about entrepreneurship. One was a thinker, the other a speculator.

- "If this facility of providing for the support of the laborer had been followed by a fall in the value of labor." The logical conclusion of this statement is that the more productive entrepreneurs and workers as a whole become, the *less* workers would be remunerated.

The "solution" is fourfold:

- Destroy the machinery (this is what primitive trade unions did).
- Destroy the entrepreneurs (this is what Marxists did).
- Destroy the "excess" workers (this is what Hitler and Stalin did).
- Make workers waste most of their lives in useless activities (this is what Keynesianism does).

Of course, this is the reasoning behind Marx assertion: "The more the division of labor and the application of machinery extend, the more does the competition extend among the *workers*, the more their wages *shrink* together." Or "the production of too many useful things results in *too many useless people*."

And consider Keynes's assertion: "Pyramid building, earthquakes and even wars may serve to *increase wealth*."

Most importantly, this is the bases if the "lump of labor fallacy" extensively elaborated by Keynes as we shall see in Chapter 5

3. "A rise in wages, from the circumstance of the laborer being more liberally rewarded, or from the difficulty of procuring the necessaries on which wages are expended does not, except in some instances, produce the effect of raising price, but has a great effect in lowering profits."

We are told that wages can be raised only by the increased generosity of the employer (it follows that this generosity can be *encouraged* in no uncertain terms) or because the cost of living went up. Nothing could be further from the truth, but that does not deter governments all over the world from constantly meddling with labor relations, causing no end of suffering for those they intend to help.

4. "has a great effect in lowering profits"

To put an end to this drivel, we need to establish once and for all what determines the price of labor—that is, the wage. The price of labor is determined by the interaction of

- an employer who wants to pay *whatever it takes* to secure the services of the staff she needs *and no more* and
- a worker who wants the job and wants the best deal she can get.

Few employers would pay a worker more than what they expect to obtain in terms of additional profits as a result of hiring him. But this puts an upper limit, not a price, on labor.

Supply and demand—not the liberality of the employer or the cost of necessities or any combination of them—determines the wage.

The price of labor is determined by two elements: supply and demand.
Nothing more, nothing less, nothing else.

Force or the threat of the use of force can, from time to time may be used by trade union leaders or populist governments. These actions may force salaries above or below the level the market would have arrived at on its own, but this cannot go too far or remain in place for too long.

The argument that "a rise in wages has a great effect in lowering profits" lacks any foundation in reality, but is designed to elicit a specific reaction among both employers (based on this information, they would fight any improvement in working conditions as a matter of principle) and workers (who should see the "struggle" as a zero-sum game). Marx and the catastrophic industrial relations that plagued Britain and America for one hundred years, follow.

Reality bears little connection with this nonsense: employers do not liberally reward workers, nor do they generally increase salaries because the cost of necessities has gone up. They increase salaries because they have to, either because competition for workers is increasing or because new or increased business requires workers fast.

In the first case, the increased cost of labor is simply a new piece of information that will change the economics of investing on labor-saving devices or leaving lines of business that are hopelessly out of sync with the market. For example, labor-intensive prawn farming in Switzerland may not be a good idea, but in certain parts of India it can be very profitable for all involved. In the second case, the employer is clearly expecting better business and better profits, and that is why she is happy to pay extra.

5. "Taxes on those commodities which are generally denominated luxuries fall only on those who make use of them. But taxes on necessaries do not affect the consumers of necessaries in proportion to the quantity that may be consumed by them, but often in a much higher proportion."

Whatever raises the wages of labor (remember that in the Ricardian world, salaries follow the cost of living) lowers the profits of stock.

6. "A tax on the necessaries of the laborer that would raise wages lowers the profits of stock; therefore every tax on any commodity consumed by the laborer has a tendency to lower the rate of profits."

This is the basis of the exorbitant taxation of all commodities in Europe, which starts at 15 percent and can get much higher once all other taxes are added. In doing this, we believe we are taxing the profits of stock. Of course Ricardo starts with "taxes on luxuries," but over time everything is a luxury and therefore subject to tax.

What is more, by artificially increasing the final price of a product, a significant amount of production will simply never take place. People have what they have, and they value things the way they value them. Salaries are not going to increase, because the price of things has been artificially inflated.

Ricardo did not understand the nature of taxation, and any tax policy based on Ricardian nonsense does and will produce greater economic damage than it will ever collect in revenue —an awful lot of pain for very little gain.

7. "With regard to a tax on raw product [pretty much the only thing laborers consumed in the Ricardian world], it appears to me that no interval which could bear oppressively on the laborer would elapse between the rise in the price of raw produce and the rise in the wages of the laborer, and that no other inconvenience would be suffered by this class." And "a tax on corn does not necessarily diminish the quantity of corn; it only raises its money price."

By claiming that "no interval which could bear oppressively on the laborer will elapse between the rise in the price of raw produce and the rise in wages of the laborer" Ricardo is telling governments that they can increase the cost of living through taxation as much as they want, because employers will pick the tab. Nothing could be further from the truth as third generation welfare recipients can testify.

8. "Taxes on wages will raise wages, and therefore diminish the rate of the profits of stock."

This is the rationale behind the regressive tax on job creation we call Social Security contributions. Taxes on wages reduce the number of people employed and reduce the take-home salary of those who remain in employment. Nothing else.
But it gets worse. Just keep reading.

9. "'A man is rich or poor,' says Adam Smith, 'according to the degree in which he can afford to enjoy the necessaries, conveniences and amusements of human life.'"
   "Value then essentially differs from riches, for value depends not on abundance, but on the difficulty or facility of production."

Here we are told (again) that the only driving force in human affairs is envy. This is patently false since many people are also driven by sloth, wrath, greed, pride, gluttony, lust or combinations thereof.

10. "The labor of a million men in manufactures will always produce the same value but will not always produce the same riches. By the invention of machinery, by improvements in skill, by a better division of labor, or the discovery of new markets, where more advantageous exchanges can be made, a million men may produce double or treble the amount of riches, of "necessaries, conveniences and amusements," in one state of society than they could produce in another, but they will not on that account add anything to value; for everything rises or falls in value in proportion to the facility or difficulty of producing it, or, in other words, in proportion to the quantity of labor employed in its production."

Now, this one is not for the faint of heart. Ricardo defines riches as "the necessaries, conveniences and amusements of life," which is correct. He does not define *value* in this paragraph but makes it dependent on the difficulty or facility of production. It follows that new riches add nothing to value.

But if riches add nothing to value because "everything rises or falls in value in proportion to the facility or difficulty of producing it" it is not riches—that is, the abundance of good food, good clothing, good housing, education, leisure, and so on—that adds value but *something else*.

That something else is enforced equality: if we can all afford more things just because they are cheaper, the social structure remains unchanged. We all live better, but the differences remain and envy, the only important element in the Ricardian world, cannot be assuaged.

This is plainly false: The quality of life of the kings and queens of England didn't change much from 1500 to 1600 to 1700 to 1800 to 1900 or to 2000. The quality of life of the lower classes has changed for the better beyond all recognition.

Ricardo assumes that *envy* is the only thing that matters and that assuaging envy is the only purpose of government action—that no one really cares about his own or his family's quality of life, but of their rung in the pecking order. This is nonsense, and it was even more nonsensical when Ricardo was writing; envy was still a sin, not the favorite prop in the reformers' bag of tricks.

Millions of citizens of the Third World leave middle-class existence to become working class in the developed world. It is quality of life and hope for the future, not social-status that motivates them. Not all people are prone to envy. Far from it: workers had to be made envious by the unrelenting pamphleteering. They still do.

People have to be reminded constantly that even if they are doing extremely well, others *may be* doing better. And that permanent—or rather permanently enforced and reinforced—grudge against society can be assuaged only by more politicians, more civil servants, more government agencies, more regulation, more taxes, and more handouts to ensure that "better distribution" is achieved.

11. "I say excepting for a limited period, because no point is better established, than that the supply of laborers will always ultimately be in proportion to the means of supporting them."

We've heard this nonsense so many times by now, that it seems innocuous and even plausible. Ricardo lifted this statement from his friend Malthus, a low-ranking priest turned economist who wrote a hilarious (I mean, really I was in stitches when I read it) book titled *An Essay on Population*. In it he aims to demonstrate that in hunter-gatherer societies, the population always ebbs and flows in line with the food provided by nature, in other words "the means of supporting them". The amount of food available may vary wildly from year to year—that is, a particularly hot, cold, dry, or wet season can have an enormous impact on both the food supply and the population.

There is no way to extend the concept of "means of supporting them" to a capitalist industrial economy. No. Here Ricardo is answering Adam Smith. Smith told us that the accumulation of capital was good for two reasons:

    a. *utilitarian* because by increasing demand for labor it raised real salaries and improved the lot of the masses (and obviously provided employment to extra workers) and

    b. *social* (or "moral"), because the larger the accumulation of capital the lower the returns the capitalist could expect for her money.

"The increase in capital, which raises wages, tends to lower profit."

So, we all have to work less to get more, except the capitalist, who has to work more to get less. No, says Ricardo, the lot of the working masses can never be improved unless their numbers are cut down well below the means of supporting them.

This is not a rant against capitalism but against life itself. We are not told who, but presumably it is the politicians or civil servants who are to decide who will live and who will die. (The Soviet Union for example, was not only a slave camp; it was also an extermination camp.)

The idea that humans are vermin is not new; it can be traced back to the eighteenth century to a low-ranking priest and a high-school dropout.

The European race is likely to become the first ethnic group ever to be exterminated by liberalism. Japan and China may follow suit.

Will we stop this death cult in time? Liberalism and its alternatives—socialism, communism, Keynesianism, welfarism—are all medicines from the same laboratory, and they all produce the same side effect: extermination, first of the best and then of the rest.

Maybe all we can aspire to is to warn all the races who have not embarked on this road to the grave—Indians, Arabs, Turks, Southeast Asians, Brazilians, Africans—not to get started.

    12. "The opinion that the price of commodities depends solely on the proportion of supply to demand or demand to supply has become almost

an axiom in political economy and has been the *source of much error* in that science."

At risk of sounding condescending I honestly believe that David Ricardo's writings are the *source of much, maybe most, error in that science*. As for his main contention, I haven't come across a better explanation for prices than the interactions of suppliers and buyers in the market, and I don't know of anyone who has.

12. "The employment of machinery could never be safely discouraged in a state, for if a capital is not allowed to get the greatest net revenue that the use of machinery will afford here, it will be carried abroad, and this must be a much more serious discouragement to the demand for labor than the most extensive employment of machinery; for while a capital is employed in this country it must create a demand for some labor; machinery cannot be worked without the assistance of men, it cannot be made but with the contribution of their labor. By investing part of a capital in improved machinery there will be a diminution in the progressive demand for labor; by exporting it to another country the demand will be wholly annihilated."

Where do we start?

First, the employment of machinery *should be discouraged* but can never be done safely.

Second, that improved machinery leads to a diminution in the *progressive* demand for labor. (It was obvious even then that the use of machinery increased the demand for labor. By using the word *progressive*, he means to say—less than it would otherwise have been—an absurd statement that can neither be proven nor disproved.) American Liberal politicians blame machinery even today as the cause of unemployment.

Third, investment overseas destroys demand for labor at home, regardless of what the investment may be. (Keynes was to transform this nonsense into a matter of dogma.)

Modern politicians' threats to companies who invest overseas prove that bad ideas refuse to die, particularly when they are part of the curricula.

Conclusion

I have been marginally unfair to Ricardo. At the end of the day, he was just an amateur talking from *his own interpretation of other people's interpretations* of economic phenomena.

He should have never been taken seriously.

The world would be a better place if David Ricardo had never started writing. Exorcising his bizarre and destructive ideas from the modern mind is an ongoing challenge for those of us who genuinely care about our fellow humans.

To them, the will, the wish, the want, the liberty, the toil and the blood of individuals is nothing. Individuality is left out of their scheme of government, the state is all in all, everything is referred to the production of force; afterwards, everything is trusted to the use of it, it is military in its principle, in its maxims, in its spirit and in all its movements, the state has dominion and conquest for its sole objects dominion over minds by proselytism, over bodies, by arms.

EDMUND BURKE

CHAPTER 4

WHY SOCIALIST ECONOMIES FAIL

We are always amused when socialists of all shades try to explain why socialism never really works: people are *not* better off by disposing of the entrepreneurial class, as socialists promised, while inequality increases exponentially.

We get two distinct groups of answers: happy-go-lucky socialists (those who want to live in paradise and believe the civil service can provide it) claim that "the people are not ready" or "the people are too stupid/ignorant/selfish." Those who know full well what socialism entails, argue correctly that to do away with all the liberties and privileges of a free people, one needs to proceed slowly, one bit at a time, until there is no living memory of any fruitful exercise of freedom.

The former are what Lenin allegedly called "the useful innocents." The latter are the socialist political and media elite, which may contain useful innocents but not very many or very often or for very long. Both groups are equally deluded: the useful innocents soon find out that socialism is anything but paradise, while the intellectual elite soon find that the bullet, the concentration camp, and the torture chambers—not *intellect* or *reason*—drives socialist dystopias.

In trying to untangle the morass of left-wing thinking, one faces the apparently insurmountable problem that there are no clear-cut, agreed-on definitions of what socialism actually is. There are about as many versions of socialism as there are socialists—and maybe more, since even non-socialists have their own definitions.

What most of them do have in common is a number of beliefs:

- Capitalism unfairly concentrates power and wealth among small segments of society.
- Those segments of society control capital and derive their wealth through the exploitation of workers.
- This creates an *unequal* society.
- This *unequal* society does not provide equal opportunities for everyone to maximize their potential.
- Capitalists do not use technology and resources neither to their full potential nor in the interest of the many.
- Either partial or total state or social (worker) control of the means of production, distribution, and exchange can remedy these deficiencies.

Here we concern ourselves with the economics of socialism, including the mild form known as the mixed economy.

Socialism is a totalitarian ideology; this means that no aspect of human life is left outside the reach of government. Isolating the economic aspects from the legal, social, cultural, and personal aspects is not as simple as it sounds, but we will do our best.

ECONOMICS AND SOCIALISM

1. Capitalism unfairly concentrates power and wealth among small segments of society.

From the dawn of time governments the world over have strived to keep both the political *and* the economic power in their own hands.

The result is a type of poverty, backwardness, and oppression difficult to imagine in a capitalist country: the same guy on whose graces you depend for employment, food, lodging, and everything else is the guy who controls the legislative and the judiciary, the police and the criminal underworld. No one outside a tiny number of interconnected families has any say, power, freedom, or hope.

The largely Venetian constitution of Britain from 1688 to 1928 changed all that: people could pursue their industry without government patronage or control. This enabled a new class of individuals who were not government officials and were not members of the aristocracy to make their money and to have some say in the running of the place. Most importantly, it gave them the independent means to pursue their aims, to campaign, to proselytize, and to discuss in a way the mendicant-like commercial class in the rest of the world could not, even today.

To the conservative, the idea of vast fortunes divorced from social duty is a matter of concern. (The spectacle of socialist billionaires popping in and out of the White House springs to mind.)

At the beginning of this process of "liberation" very few people saw a return to the previous stage—that is, the combination of political and economic power in the hands of a hereditary elite (and rest assured that bureaucratic and political powers become hereditary as soon as the economy begins to tank), as a solution to any perceived problem.

But this process of medievalist reaction, which began in 1755 with the publication of Morelly's *Code of Nature* and reached fever pitch with the publication in 1848 of Karl Marx and Friedrich Engel's *Communist Manifesto*, could not capture the imagination of the masses, who knew all too well just how much their lot had been improved by capitalism.

It would take many decades of compulsory education in the hands of the state to instill in the minds of the people the idea that if civil servants and politicians were granted the control of the whole of the economy—on top of controlling the executive, the legislative, the judiciary, the education system, the media, the police, the army, and the security apparatus—they could and *would* use such power to improve the lot of the common citizen. Human naivety knows no bounds.

A most astonishing realization was awaiting the socialist enthusiasts: they knew or ought to have known—Marx had said it in as many words—that competitive capitalism had ushered in more material progress in one hundred years than government controls had in the previous six thousand. They were about to find out that the political machinery that had failed to create economic progress for six thousand years running was also incapable of maintaining it. Moreover, this inability was not accidental nor could it be remedied.

Here is why: a successful enterprise is constantly pulled apart by the competing forces of suppliers (who are always demanding better terms for themselves), workers (who want to be paid as much as possible), management (who usually have their own agenda), politicians (who want an ever larger share of the profits in the form of taxation), community activists (who are constantly demanding freebies), and customers trying to get the most for the least amount of money, among many others.

Only the desire, the determination, the discipline, and the dedication of businesspeople keep the show on the road *despite* all these stakeholders. These stakeholders, while having a vaguely defined common interest in the survival and success of the organization, have an individual interest in getting the best deal for themselves and have no way of knowing—or any reason for caring about—how much they endanger the organizational whole through their actions.

Politicians and civil servants have no reason to subject themselves to the stress of the entrepreneur. As natural-born compromisers, they are better off either aligning themselves with a particular group or playing one group against the other for personal gain.

Torn between very strong forces and with nothing to gain from their own success, the management of nationalized industries simply takes it easy and waits for retirement while their organizations implode or have to be continually rescued by the government.

But it gets worse: politicians not used to being rebuked by the electorate (which is entirely dependent on the political class for survival) have no reason for even pretending to do a good job in the running of the country.

The concentration of both political and economic power in one set of hands is about as bad for politics as it is for economics. It is not progress; it is retrogression. It's not revolution; it is a brutal, misguided, and suicidal *reaction* against progress.

As for the concentration of wealth and power, only an electorate that is not dependent on the state and a political class for its survival can vote into office individuals who can stand up to the encroachments of the state bureaucracy on one hand and the financial, commercial and industrial elite on the other. Such an electorate can come into existence only in a successful economy abounding in jobs, goods, and services, and never in a state-controlled one.

Merging political and economic power is guaranteed to achieve exclusively what the socialist hopes to avoid: poverty and inequality.

2. Those segments of society control capital and derive their wealth though exploitation.

As anyone who has seen taxes raised again and again, entire industries regulated out of existence, or trade unions paralyzing cities and even countries could tell you, those who control—or more precisely, those who *deploy* capital in a productive manner—are often the victims of arbitrary power and exploitation. It seems that as soon as the capital is deployed—and visible—it becomes an object of envy and passes to the hands of the collective.

Now the idea of exploitation presents some difficulties. Exploitation literally means the productive working or profitable management of mines, cattle or other natural resources. Commonly used in the context of mining and agriculture, it gives the idea of taking something out without any form of reparation or compensation.

Again, from a moral point of view—assuming morals have anything to do with mining or herding—the implications tend to be negative.

The term *exploitation* was only too tempting for people arguing that workers are being taken advantage of since they do not receive in payment what they produce through their labor. This is true: workers do not receive from the entrepreneur what they would produce without the entrepreneur— *they receive more,* otherwise they would be self-employed. Compare the quality of life of a Western or Japanese worker with that of a self-employed man in any pre-capitalist country.

The use of the word *exploitation* was supposed to stir the mind of the working masses toward revolutionary upheaval. It never did: workers inhabit the real world, intellectuals do not.

3. This creates an unequal society.

Socialism finds its roots in utilitarianism or "the greatest happiness for the greatest number." The materialism of Marx and Engels determined that happiness should be defined by material comforts—rather, the *equality* of material comforts or lack thereof.

It is nothing short of astonishing that equality or more precisely the quest for equality −which is largely a device designed to simultaneously stir *and* soothe the feeling of envy− could ever become a rallying cry for socialists the world over.

An ideology that denies the existence of needs that are not material suddenly decides that a particular *feeling* (envy) not only deserves government attention but should become the cornerstone of all policymaking. Why not other feelings, such as lust or indolence? Or family, community, spirituality, or national belonging? It's difficult to tell.

The best explanation I find is economic: if equality of living conditions becomes the dominant or the only driving force in society, it follows that the main or even the only task of the government bureaucracy and political class is to take from those who have and to give to those who don't.

Taking from those who have is a logistical impossibility, as any socialist billionaire would tell you; they are just too clever and too well advised to fall for it. Often the most valuable thing they have is their own talents.

Then the only alternative is taking from those who earn, but this also presents problems, as serious earners are almost always those who have and therefore are out of the reach of the politicians and bureaucrats.

All that is left is to take from those who work and to give the proceeds to those who don't. This system of permanent redistribution achieves quite a few transitional objectives:

- It gives an overall, unquestionable direction to the state.
- It allows the state to employ millions of civil servants, who would otherwise be employed in productive endeavors that could lead to wealth creation, capital formation, and better lives for all, reducing the appeal of socialism.
- It creates a permanent and ever-expanding underclass of welfare recipients that can be manipulated for political purposes.
- It prevents capital formation in the hands of anyone who is not already rich or politically connected.
- It forces those who work for a living to work much longer and for lower pay.
- Over time it requires many more compulsions to be kept going: extortionate taxation combined with myriad regulations in the life of the worker on the one hand and complete, minute control of the lives of the welfare recipients on the other.

This system does not produce overall equality; instead it produces *equality among equals*: all those individuals who are not part of the political, financial, and intellectual elite. Workers, welfare recipients, entrepreneurs, professionals and the self-employed are *equalized*.

Equality for the masses; liberty and fraternity for the classes.

Once it is set in motion, this constant process of fiscal exploitation, impoverishment, and erosion of liberty tends to have no end. *There is no lower limit to human degradation.*

Now, if an unequal society is a problem, the equal society should be the solution. But even if one is happy to overlook the fact that socialist arrangements not only fail to promote equality but make societies ostensibly polarized, it is obvious that an equal society has never existed and will never exist, and for one very good reason: survival.

Humans are different in physical abilities, intellectual abilities, moral abilities, courage, birth, wealth, charms, connections, sex, gender, race, and age, to name but a few. The survival and the progress of civilization require all such diversity and more. But there is a catch: abilities are not enough. Desire, determination, discipline, and dedication are the only way to push those innate or acquired abilities and talents to their limits and to make them useful.

The impossibility of making it big—that is, to be financially unequal—drives the attention of an entrepreneurial mind toward other equally rewarding endeavors, chiefly politics and civil service. The problem with this is an extraordinary waste of talent. What use is a guy who employs his talents and abilities to become head of a government department when he could have gone into business and employed thousands by producing new goods and services people wanted or needed?

Those who are keen to sacrifice liberty to achieve equality usually find themselves unfree and unequal.

4. This unequal society does not provide equal opportunities for everyone to maximize their potential.

This is designed specifically to attract those who believe themselves to have great potential but have no intention of realizing it. No social and economic arrangement except free, capitalist, democratic societies has ever produced or will ever produce more opportunities—or just as importantly, incentives— for everyone to maximize their potential. These arrangements have enormous rewards for those who get out there and do things and more modest rewards for those who are happy to take a contemplative approach to life. The result is that millions of people who spend their lives thinking fail to achieve financially what less intellectually curious but more enterprising individuals do. Socialism promises a paradise for the intellectual, in which they will be top dog and where learning takes center stage. This is, of course, a fantasy.

Socialism leads to a shrinking economy and less of everything for everyone. In their quest to retain wealth and status, the socialist ruling classes retain all the best jobs and positions for their own people, simultaneously removing the opportunities to maximize potential *and* any incentives to do so for the rest of the population. For the intellectual, there is the ration card, the concentration camp and ultimately, an early grave.

5. Technology and resources are not used by capitalists, either to their full potential or in the interest of the many.

This is part gimmick and part self-delusion. Entrepreneurs go into business to produce the goods and to provide the services people *may want to buy* (this is never certain beforehand) at a cost lower than the prices people *may be happy to pay*. While it is debatable whether businesses are really there to maximize anything in particular, they are definitely not out there to maximize the use of technology or the use of resources but to maximize the *benefits* extracted from them (as measured by people's desire to purchase their products).

There is a very good reason for this: the idea of maximizing technology and resources is meaningless. How do you maximize railway technology? By buildings train lines to nowhere in the most difficult terrain, only to show you can? By providing spectacular services no one wants or can afford?

How do you maximize agricultural resources? By producing as much food as possible and then burning it? How do you maximize human resources? By giving individuals more responsibility than would be prudent?

This is designed to appeal to all those individuals who have grand plans yet never try to make them happen; they prefer to dream of the wonderful things that could have been, if only they had been given unlimited cash and power.

Free people will not use technology or resources if the cost of using them exceeds the value assigned to their products by those who are expected to work to pay for them. But it provides every incentive to make their use widespread and profitable, as the past three hundred years of history amply demonstrate.

6. Either partial or total state or social (worker) control of the means of production, distribution and exchange could remedy these deficiencies.

Economic arrangements based on any or all of the assumptions listed above are likely over time to reduce economic output at or even below the subsistence level, which is the ultimate equilibrium level of any economy. Any attempt to extract greater economic output under such conditions would require the use of force, since no rewards can be given for extra effort.

As we saw in point one above, political and governmental authorities are incapable of creating or maintaining an industrial economy at anything like the levels of output obtained by voluntary, for-profit cooperation.

Whichever way you chose to define it, socialism creates myriad problems of its own without resolving any of the problems of a free society. It is time to let go.

The mixed economy

So-called mixed economies address all of the points raised by the socialists (without ever questioning them). But since socialism is a reaction against liberty, prosperity, and the rule of law, any compromise—including the mixed economy—will curtail our liberty, reduce our prosperity, and undermine the rule of law for political expediency.

The mixed economy is a slower road to financial ruin and social disintegration, but the apparent lack of speed should not confuse the observer as to the final destination.

So how does the mixed economy address socialist objections to liberty, prosperity, and the rule of law?

1. Capitalism unfairly concentrates power and wealth among small segments of society.

Both state and public (shareholder) ownership remove the figure of the capitalist but also separate management from ultimate responsibility. Conglomerates become simply the playground of the well-connected and end up serving almost exclusively the interests of the senior management, their bankers, and on occasion the trade union involved.

This often complete lack of commitment and responsibility became patently obvious in the run-up to the banking crisis, in which family-run institutions did very well, publicly listed institutions did poorly, and public-sector-owned institutions did appallingly.

There is no substitute for private, individual ownership, only compromises.

2. Those segments of society control capital and derive their wealth through exploitation.

Successful attempts to raise salaries constantly and to improve working conditions have priced tens of millions of people out of the job market—particularly the young, the old, and the not-so-well connected. Since the best way to get *a good job* is to have *a job*, many of those excluded will simply never be employed. This has disastrous effects not only on the beneficiaries (that is, the victims) of welfare legislation but also on those who are employed and constantly in fear of losing their jobs.

3. This creates an unequal society.

As power is concentrated in the state, opportunities are also concentrated. Plum jobs are almost exclusively reserved for the well connected, creating the most hideous form of inequality: one not based on ability or effort but on connections, cunning, and often, criminality.

4. This unequal society does not provide equal opportunities for everyone to maximize their potential.

Opportunities are created by growing economies and expanding job markets. Absent both, most people have to settle for what they can. Highly ambitious individuals still find and exploit the limited opportunities available, but this is unlikely to help society or to be within reach of the many.

5. Technology and resources are not used by capitalist, either to their full potential or in the interest of the many.

As we have seen time and again, technology (of which managerial technology is an important example) is greatly impeded by government action, which tends to favor special interests over the general public.

Socialist regimes are very adept to making outlandish displays of financial and technological prowess. Such displays, however, are only made for propaganda reasons and rarely if ever for the benefit of the people of the country.

6. Either partial or total state or social (worker) control of the means of production, distribution, and exchange could remedy these deficiencies.

This is simple economic and political illiteracy: either the state or the workers behave like a capitalist and succeed, or they don't.

The so called mixed-economy is a slower road to self-destruction, but just like in the case of socialism, an ideology founded on the dual pillars of economic illiteracy and pathological envy is unlikely to provide answers to our problems.

What little he said that is true is not original. What little he said that is original is not true. And a lot of what he said that is not true is not original neither.

ANONYMOUS

KARL MARX

Karl Marx (1818–1883) has been hailed by some as a prophet on par with Jesus and Muhammad while his works the *Communist Manifesto* and *Das Kapital* have been called the creed and the Bible of Communism, respectively.

Marx is the man every conservative loves to hate, not because of what he wrote (he was more reactionary than any conservative that has ever existed), but because of what he was: an ungrateful, spoiled, middle-class brat who—after receiving the finest education money could buy at the time (in the agricultural region of Western Europe that was to become Germany a few decades later)— chose a parasitical life, living off his parents and friends and subjecting himself and his immediate family to extreme privations, despite the enormous handouts he received. His few surviving children entered into suicide pacts with their spouses and killed themselves early in life.

The only difference between Marx and the millions of ungrateful, spoiled, middle-class brats we so love to hate is this: they largely concern themselves with getting back at Mom and Dad, and occasionally soiling public spaces while camping in them. Marx was slightly more ambitious.

His grasp of economics was patchy at the best of times. In the dialectical form he championed, an economist summed up his economic and social thinking in the following dialogue:

KM: Workers are exploited.
Interviewer: How come?
KM: Because they are not paid what they produce.
Interviewer: Oh, and what are they paid instead?
KM: Only what they need.
Interviewer: I see. And you propose to pay them what they produce?
KM: Absolutely not.
Interviewer: What are you planning to pay them?
KM: Only what they need.

It doesn't really matter how many libraries are filled with volumes of Marxist theory, it simply never goes further than that. This is rather pathetic, since millions believe there is something more to it. As far as I know, Marx is unique among revolutionary writers, not in wanting to change everything, but in wanting to *destroy* everything to *see what happened next*. Civil war, mass starvation, millions of deaths... To have a look.

The root of the Marxist confusion comes straight from eighteenth-century thinking, in particular David Hume's contention that no special characteristics differentiate entrepreneurs from other workers. Smith goes as far as stating that the only difference between a worker and an entrepreneur is "habit."

Marx goes yet another step further: if the entrepreneur is unnecessary, he should be destroyed.

In his introduction to the Gateway edition of *Das Kapital*, Serge Levitsky gives us a glimpse of Marx's ominous work:

> Having in the Communist Manifesto assured the workers that capitalism was doomed and that the future belonged to them, Marx owed the world a more solid proof of his assertions.
> Das Kapital claims to do just that.
> The task which Marx set himself was an ambitious one. His goal was nothing less than the discovery of the economic laws of motion of modern society, and to show these laws assured the eventual triumph of the proletariat....
> The result was a curious amalgamation of economic and political theory, history, sociology and utopia.

Marx, in effect, attempted to unite all the philosophical, scientific, and moral strands of the Victorian age into one vast system of a universal scope.

Marx's method was not that of observation and scientific deduction. It was rather that of an a-priori conceptual scheme, supplemented by a wealth of documentary material selected to fit the main tenets of the scheme.

He contends:

1. The social class he calls the proletariat (that is, blue collar workers specifically engaged in production) produce more wealth that they actually enjoy.
2. The difference is enjoyed by another class: the capitalist, by virtue of its ownership of the means of production, distribution, and exchange.
3. This system is doomed, as it depends for its survival on absolute freedom of competition, which capitalism tends to eliminate. (Why? We are not told.)
4. The organization and supervision of labor, trading, transporting, wholesaling, retailing, and financing (and those agents involved in the process) add no value at all.
5. When capitalist society is overthrown, the worker will retain the full value produced by him.
6. Competition forces the capitalist to employ more efficient and more productive machinery. This in turn increases the misery of the workers.
7. This drive toward ever-increasing production—and concomitant exploitation—is not inherent in human nature, but is imposed by a class structure that compels individuals to act in their self-interest.
8. This process of accumulation and consequent exploitation will continue until the wrath of the workers leads them to overturn society.
9. The discipline of capitalist production will provide the tools and that the "growing inherent contradictions" of capitalism will spell its doom.
10. Private property will be abolished.
11. The dictatorship of the proletariat will replace capitalist society.

Levitsky continues:

It was this ethical and messianic character of Marx's theory which gave *Das Kapital* a power capable of driving people to the barricades.

It was a doctrine of deliverance of the proletariat (a myth of a class with which Marx himself had no bond or contact) what made *Das Kapital* a bible of technological messianism.

Marx endowed his theories with the double attribute of universality and inevitability.

Pro captu lectoris habent sua fata libelli
(the fate of a book is in the hands of its readers)

I would like to add another point of view: the practical point of view. Few politicians and even fewer ordinary citizens would spend the time required to understand history, politics, philosophy, theology, and economics. But few students of any discipline and even fewer professional politicians can resist the temptation of reading the twenty-page long *Communist Manifesto*, in which Marx presents a very peculiar version of history, politics, philosophy, theology, and economics, designed to lead the reader toward his conclusions.

For many, this is the only contact they will ever have with any one of these disciplines, and throughout their lives they will find themselves reaching the same absurd conclusions over and over again, without even knowing where they come from.

The *Communist Manifesto* is the ultimate meme.

The *Manifesto* is the most fiendish display of genius of the second millennium. It took only a handful of committed and well-organized terrorists to set up the network of slave and extermination camps that went by the name Communist Bloc for the better part of the twentieth century.

Just like human life, civilization is remarkably fragile.

WHAT DID MARX ACTUALLY SAY?

He started by praising capitalism in glowing terms:

* "The industrial and commercial middle class during its rule of scarce one hundred years has created more colossal productive forces than have all preceding generations together."

- "Into their place [state controls] stepped free competition, accompanied by a social and political constitution adapted to it, and the economic and political sway of the middle class."
- "The industrial middle class cannot exist without constantly revolutionizing the instruments of production."
- "By the rapid improvement of all instruments of production, by the immensely facilitated means of communication, draws all, even the most barbarous nations into civilization."

He quickly tired of all this, however, and declared, "The middle class is unfit any longer to be the ruling class in society." Why? We are not told.

He was absolutely right that capitalism had—in material terms—accomplished more in one hundred years than all the do-gooders in the previous five thousand.

- Ninety-five to 98 percent of the population, which had spent the previous five thousand years tied to the land and the seasons, suddenly could be productive all year 'round (for the first time ever).
- They could all be paid in cash (for the first time ever).
- They could buy with their cash whatever they wanted (for the first time ever).
- They were free to run their own households (for the first time ever).
- They could all live in towns or cities if they chose (for the first time ever).
- They were free to migrate and to buy land (for the first time ever).
- Women could earn a living doing something other than domestic service or prostitution (for the first time ever).
- For the working classes, it made economic sense to learn to read and write (for the first time ever).

In sum, for the first time ever the world was full of possibilities. Many people were desperate to take advantage of them, and many did. That this was going to trigger a backlash should have come as no surprise.

However, the backlash was not going to come from the working classes, who, using Marx's own words, could be easily bribed with higher salaries and better living conditions (yes, please!). It would come from the over-educated scions of the middle classes (such as Marx, Engels, Lenin, Trotsky, Guevara to name but a few), who were unwilling to become productive workers. They saw all their intellect and learning going to waste as both entrepreneurs and workers went on living without any regard for their enlightened opinions.

The phenomenon of the socialist/Marxist intellectual "elite" is still with us today. It has demanded and obtained millions of unnecessary bureaucratic posts— elected or otherwise—political posts, and academic posts. It enjoys the best working conditions, the highest salaries, the earliest (and most remunerative) retirements, the longest holidays, and the lowest levels of stress of any class of workers.

Of course, this is because they and only they can be trusted with protecting *the proletariat*. Or rather because it is they and only they who should be feared.

How did they achieve that? Marx gives us his methodology in the shape of "Ten Commandments" of communism

1. Abolition of [the right to own] property in land and application of all rents of land to public purposes
2. Heavy progressive or graduated income taxes
3. Abolition of all rights of inheritance
4. Confiscation of the property of all emigrants and rebels
5. Centralization of credit in the hands of the state, by means of a national bank with state capital and an exclusive monopoly
6. Centralization of the means of communication and transport in the hands of the state
7. Extension of factories and instruments of production owned by the state, the cultivation of wastelands, and the improvement of the soil generally in accordance with a common plan
8. Equal obligation of all to work and establishment of industrial armies, especially for agriculture
9. Combination of agriculture with manufacturing industries and gradual abolition of all the distinctions between town and country through a more equable distribution of the population over the country
10. Free education for all children in public schools as well as abolition of children's factory labor and the combination of education with industrial production, etc.

Writing these as ten commandments was a stroke of genius. There isn't a single commandment that hasn't been implemented totally or partially around the world. What is not in the statute books is often proposed by one politician or another.

These policy tools are already such a permanent feature of the political and economic landscape that the reader may be wondering what is wrong with them. We see it only when we are confronted with the rationale behind them:

- to foster the disappearance of class distinctions, and
- to enable "the sweeping away by force of old (that is, the new) conditions of production," so that
- power can "lose its political character."

Then the whole scheme begins to make sense, namely,

The disappearance of class distinctions is —apparently—a most remarkable display of naivety; replacing the old entrepreneurial class will require a vast, unwieldy bureaucracy, which will almost by definition become the new ruling class.

When we look at the results, however, we quickly realize that this was part of the plan from the beginning (no naivety involved). What little is left of the old entrepreneurial spirit after confiscation, exorbitant taxation, regulation, and so on could never be a match for the new masters of society, who reign supreme and proceed unchallenged as they "Sweep away by force of old conditions of production"—that is, the running to the ground of all our industrial capabilities.

Finally, power will "lose its political character"—that is, once all the power has been concentrated in the political and bureaucratic class, the new class structure of society would be the state and "the rest." The bureaucracy would have only one objective: the acquisition, the exercise, the retention, and the expansion of power by any means.

Intellectual and ideological diversity –party politics–, which is what Marx refers to when he talks of "political character," would become redundant: the state-run education system would produce only one type of individual, one that looks up to the state for everything.

Sounds familiar?

Marx and his followers present us not with a class struggle as such but with an intra-class struggle—namely, whether the entrepreneurial element of the middle class or the intellectual element of the middle class (the politician, the civil servant... Marx) who rules the roost.

The tragedy in all this is that politicians, bureaucrats, and well-established entrepreneurs (which in most countries are members of the same families) will eventually find mutual accommodation to the detriment of both the working classes and the real intellectual elite (the elite of brains and talents, not of family connections). A world of desperation for the poor and of spiritual, intellectual, and cultural mediocrity for all will be the result of this most unholy alliance between those with *unearned influence* and those with *unearned wealth*.

Marx's ultimate goal—the complete destruction of Western world—is not in itself an economic plan. The economy is just the tool.

Let's see how the commandments achieve these objectives:

1. Abolition of [the right to own] property in land and application of all rents of land to public purposes

The abolition of property in land can only mean the transfer of property first to the state and then to politicians and civil servants turned oligarchs. The purpose of this policy is not food production but the uprooting of the largely conservative elements of rural population. Uprooted agricultural workers, often political prisoners, are a poor substitute for the no-nonsense farmer.

Objective: elimination of a free, deeply principled, financially independent citizenry.

2. Heavy progressive or graduated income taxes

There are three objectives:

1. To remove all incentives to economic progress (especially social mobility) among the working classes (whose take-home pay would not increase remotely in line with their efforts, thanks to the heavy, progressive, and graduated elements of the tax), ensuring that education and with it all government jobs are retained by the intellectual middle class—that is, the likes of Marx and Engels.
2. To discourage economic activity among all those men and women of talent who do not pursue a career in the civil service (whose members are often tax exempt and whose guaranteed pensions render saving for retirement unnecessary).

3. To reduce capital formation to a minimum or even to send it into reverse, and with it job creation and the emergence of new entrepreneurs who may challenge those already established or the power of the state bureaucracy or political class.

Objective: elimination of social mobility.

3. Abolition of all right of inheritance

Politicians and civil servants always have and always will place their children in positions of power if they so choose. The banking elite have no problems moving their billions around the world as they see fit. Everybody else, particularly industrialists and merchants (farmers having already lost their property), will have to start from scratch with each passing generation.

Objective: a return to the Bronze Age.

4. Confiscation of the property of all emigrants and rebels

If restrictions one, two, and three have not dissuaded you, anything you own will be taken away from you, either because you are seen as a rebel or because you seek to escape. The fear of total ruin by confiscation would be enough to dissuade even the most ardent lover of freedom from saying a word or standing up to the criminal communist elite. Recent threats in France and the United States to impose "special taxes" on emigrants find their origin here.

Objective: total submission of civil society to the civil service.

5. Centralization of credit in the hands of the state by means of a national bank with state capital and an exclusive monopoly

We can see this practice everywhere: bankers and entrepreneurs with all the right connections make billions at everybody else's expense, simply by tapping the central bank. Entrepreneurs without the right connections wither and die or accumulate wealth much slower than those on the government payroll.

Objective: total control over the economy by the civil service.

6. Centralization of the means of communication and transport in the hands of the state

Only friends of the government would get to say much at all. No one opposed to the government version of events would ever be allowed to talk or to write to the public—or to move around the country freely.

Objective: total control over the mind.

7. Extension of factories and instruments of production owned by the state, the cultivation of wastelands, and the improvement of the soil generally in accordance with a common plan

Objective: the state as the sole employer: as Trotsky so eloquently put it, those who do not obey shall not eat.

8. Equal obligation of all to work and establishment of industrial armies, especially for agriculture

With the person of independent means all but extinguished, there is only the bureaucracy and the individual, who now stands penniless, lonely and in fear for his life. If he still refuses to submit, he will be enslaved (obligated to work).

Objective: the elimination of all opposition, real or potential.

9. Combination of agriculture with manufacturing industries and gradual abolition of all distinctions between town and country through a more equable distribution of the population over the country

A return to Middle Ages feudalism, with the bureaucrat or party official as the feudal, hereditary lord—masters of life and death—and a hereditary presidency as we have seen in North Korea and Cuba.

Objective: small communities can be easily and cheaply controlled or, if necessary, destroyed to be made an example of.

10. Free education for all children in public schools as well as abolition of children's factory labor and the combination of education with industrial production, etc.

For this state of affairs to continue, every new generation must be taught by civil servants to see politicians and civil servants as saviors and the official version of events as undisputed and unquestionable truth. No child would ever leave school believing that liberty, prosperity, and the rule of law—or morality of any sort—are anything other than anachronistic, unsustainable absurdities.

Yet there would be schools especially designed to form the children of politicians, civil servants, and the surviving entrepreneurs, who are destined for positions of power while the rest are taught how their leaders have saved them.

Objective: to make sure that once we have returned to the Bronze Age, we don't get out.

ECONOMIC CONCLUSIONS ON MARXISM

In Marx we see the culmination of the moralizing approach to economics popularized by Adam Smith almost a century before the publication of *Das Kapital*.

While Smith is not particularly keen on the economics of liberty, but rightly concludes that only a free economy can support a free society, Marx contends that freedom is the problem. He convinces the reader that liberty is the problem that needs to be resolved, thus making loyal followers out of college students who are angry with their elders for not doing what they would have them do.

Unlike his intended readers—the British—Marx had never known liberty, and he failed to make it repugnant in the mind of the reader. That task would fall to John Maynard Keynes, who succeeded in making liberty, prosperity, and the rule of law not only repugnant but also unfashionable, anachronistic, and *unsustainable*. Marxist economics fail because they take prosperity for granted.

Amid all the moralizing and reforming, torturing, raping, and killing, Marx and his followers forgot that either in tyranny or in liberty, people still need to eat. If production, distribution, and exchange become political games, people go hungry, and then it's a matter of every man for himself.

The Western world is marching apace toward its own ruin because we—like Karl Marx before us—are also taking prosperity for granted. An ever-increasing number of American and European citizens resort to food aid. We are quite fortunate we can still provide it. Political economy today is all about change and reform and fairness and social responsibility, not output employment or opportunity for the young, the vulnerable and the not so well connected.

Our taxation has long ceased to be the means for defraying state expenditure and is increasingly a means of redressing the intangible, undefined *unfairness of it all*. In the meantime we are already talking of a lost generation: those who will never work and if they do will never enjoy the things their parents and grandparents did. Millions who never struggled are today hurting, frightened, and lonely. We have Herr Marx and his followers to thank for this.

PHILOSOPHICAL CONCLUSION ON MARXISM

Professor Russell Kirk told us,

> Despite Marx's formal adherence to utilitarian concepts of argument and proof, despite his belligerent determination to be *scientific*, his influence has been that of a *man of imagination* —an imagination begrimed and fettered, true, but still participating in the world of ideas, superior to the tyranny of particular facts.
>
> To consider whether Marx was "right" or "wrong"; to dredge Volumes I and III of *Das Kapital* for inconsistencies or logical flaws, to "refute" the Marxian system, is, in the last resort, sheer waste of time, says professor Alexander Gray; "for when we consort with Marx we are no longer in the world of reason or logic."
>
> He saw visions—clear visions of the passing of all things, much more nebulous visions of how all things may be made new.
>
> And his visions, or some of them, awoke a responsive chord in the hearts of many men.
>
> Though assertedly a materialist, in truth Marx was an idealist, indoctrinated by Hegel; and this aspect of his character, which he endeavored to strip from himself as if it were a Nessus' shirt, accounts nevertheless for his victory over the utilitarians whose method he imitated.
>
> He dealt, however mistakenly, with ends; the Liberals, with means and particulars; and the mass of men being governed by imagination more than reason, in such struggle the odds favor the visionary.
>
> **For Marx the end of human endeavor was absolute equality of condition.**
>
> He was under no illusion as to equality in a hypothetical state of nature: equality never before had existed in society, he knew, he sneered at all concepts of natural right.

Equality would be no restoration, but a creation.

Men are not equal by nature; the socialist must level them by legislation and economic device

In order to establish equality, we must first establish inequality—is this not the most significant sentence in Das Kapital?

The clever, the strong, the industrious, the virtuous, must be compelled to serve the weak and stupid and slack and vicious; nature must submit to the socialist art, so that an *idea* may be vindicated.

Gray writes, "Marx's faith in his untutored intuitions of ethical knowledge, illustrated in his unquestioning adherence to the goal of communism, his philosophy of history and his assertion of the unique efficacy of the method of revolution in social development, are examples of an apriorism which is the essence of idealism."

Arbitrary though this ethical end *equality* is, in it resides more imagination than in the endless reiteration of "the greatest happiness of the greater number." Thus the radical impulse that the liberals once employed has deserted Benthamism for Marxism.

The principle of envy, shrouded in verbiage, vanquishes naked self-interest.

Keynes was an intuitive genius. But he was not a good economist.

F. A. HAYEK

CHAPTER 5

WHY KEYNESIAN ECONOMIES FAIL

Note:When I asked friends to review this book, the conclusion was unanimous:"One cannot criticize Keynes and expect to get away with it. And certainly one does not call Keynes a Marxist without sounding like a complete lunatic." "You can go as far as explaining that his ideas do not work, because they don't, but the guy is an icon of the left, an icon of the right, a gay icon . . ." "He saved capitalism from itself. Any hint that he was a Marxist and you will be labeled a conspiracy theorist."

That left me wondering.Was he really a Marxist, as I made him out to be? (Does it matter now?) And did he really "save" capitalism, as we are taught he did, even if he did so unwittingly?

Keynes's The General Theory of Employment, Interest and Money *is an attempt to effect first national socialism and over time Soviet-style socialism, without anything like the physical violence those systems require.*

Keynes had read Marx on two occasions, according to his biographer, but he claimed to be unimpressed. It must have had some influence, since the General Theory *is a denunciation of capitalism and is so completely at odds with Keynes's writings before his reading of Marx that one could reasonably assume some sort of Damascene conversion.*

What is more, it is perfectly clear from Keynes' behavior that he thought his own ideas to be the real thing, not just a source of entertainment before the world came back to its senses (after the thirties) and went back to the System of Liberty.

Believing that total government control is the only way to do things, but eliminating the "need" for the physical extermination of the entrepreneurial class, he ensured we lived to fight another day. We will never know whether he sacrificed himself for the greater-good by pretending to believe or whether he really believed in national-socialism as the only way to save the free world.

What we can speculate is that, given the incontrovertible successes of the Soviet and the Nazi economies and the absolute failure of the economies of the free world—at least according to the press at the time—it would have been dangerous to continue to claim that liberty and the rule of law were a sure way to prosperity.

Describing John Maynard Keynes as "not a good economist," as Hayek did, may be the greatest understatement of all times. He was an intuitive genius, albeit of the kind one would rather do without. He intuitively understood three basic principles:

1. Drawing one's followers by appealing to their sense of superiority, entitlement, and importance, making them believe that they are part of a secret cabal, ensures that no amount of reason—or tangible evidence to the contrary—will make them abandon the creed.
2. The battle is for the hearts and minds—that is, for the ultimate fate of humanity. The economy is just a tool.
3. Make your ideas universal—that is, equally valid in North as in South America, in Europe as in Africa, in Japan as in Cambodia. Any opposition on the grounds of, say, reality or evidence to the contrary will be local by definition. Thus the victims are isolated from each other, while their tormentors enjoy universal brotherhood. (Marxists and other globally ambitious ideologies employed and continue to employ the same technique.)

Keynes, like Marx, was a dreamer who believed that millions of dreamers like him, cleverly deployed around the world, would *change civilization*. He was right: destruction is a form of change.

While Malthus is the root of all evil, Keynes is the true subversive: he didn't just tell the world that complete submission to the power of the state was *inevitable and desirable* (that is what Marx and Engels did); he convinced the world that rejecting such submission was *unfashionable and unscientific*, almost conservative

(God forbid), and that is the last thing any self-respecting politician, civil servant, academic, or Hollywood star wants to be called.

I intended to use a three-pronged approach to this most influential work:

1. identifying and exploring the core tenets of Keynes's philosophy, providing current examples of their application,
2. identifying all the statements that, while wholly or largely unconnected to the theory, instill in the reader a deep hatred of liberty, prosperity, and the rule of law, and a deep suspicion, disdain, and outright revulsion and contempt for all the economic and monetary arrangements that make liberty and prosperity possible, and
3. identifying the glaring contradictions that lie at the heart of the theory.

Economics is a serious business, and one should never lower the tone unduly. Keynes's contradictions are so many so funny and so embarrassing, the reader would incorrectly assume one is not approaching the subject with the rigor it deserves.

A WORD OF WARNING

While the preface of the 1936 first edition of the *General Theory of employment, interest and money*, written by Keynes himself, states that "this book is chiefly addressed to my fellow economists." Keynes was not an economist and few, if any, economists at the time would have paid much attention to his work other than as a curiosity.

Keynes was, however, addressing his work to the *future generations of economists*. These future generations would be fundamentally different from the previous ones in that they would be civil servants or aspiring civil servants, not scientists. As such, they would be happy to continue to implement a failed policy over and over again, because that is what the consensus said or what their political masters wanted. Of course, by *consensus* we mean the consensus among people trained to take Keynes's ideas as revealed truth.

With the help of Keynes, the powers that be also ensured that economists trained after the Second World War would differ from their predecessors in another crucial respect: as the science of economics became a mind game of good is bad, right is wrong, and up is down, few individuals with any sense of intellectual honesty would stick around long enough to gain a degree on the subject (thus eliminating them from the government careers that follow).

Those who stuck around long enough would fall into two distinct categories:

1. those who actually believed or convinced themselves that good is bad, right is wrong, and up is down, and
2. those who wanted positions of power in the sphere of economic policy and would answer whatever the marker of the exam wanted to read, in order to get to where they wanted to get.

The results have been dismal for both the profession (which is wholly discredited the world over) and the victims: countries upon which Keynes's ideas have been and continue to be inflicted.

The more thorough the implementation, the more catastrophic the results.

WHAT ARE KEYNES'S IDEAS?[5]*

1. The root of all evil: what's good for the goose is bad for the gander.

It is natural to suppose that the act of an individual, by which he enriches himself without apparently taking anything from anyone else, must also enrich the community as a whole. ... Those who think in this way are deceived by an optical illusion. (21)

Translation: wealth is poverty; poverty is wealth.

I placed this statement first, not only because it appears at the beginning of Keynes's *General Theory*, but also because everything that follows hangs from this basic tenet. I call this passage "the root of all evil" because once the policymaker convinces herself that wealth, not the lack of it, is the problem that needs to be resolved, all the deranged and catastrophic policies that entrench abject poverty in the midst of plenty follow just as naturally as day follows night.

The rest of the *General Theory* is a reiteration of this *principle* in every imaginable form.

Taxes that prevent capital formation, such as steeply graduated income and corporate taxes; taxes that make economic efficiency undesirable, such as capital gains taxes; taxes that get in the way of wealth creation, such as

---

[5]* All quotes are from *The General Theory of Employment Interest and Money* by John Maynard Keynes, a fellow of Kings College Cambridge (New York: Macmillan, 1949).

value-added tax; taxes that get in the way of job creation, such as Social Security contributions; environmental regulations that force manufacturing away; and transaction taxes designed to prevent economic activity—all aim to *resolve the problem of wealth*.

2. Conspiracy theory and the fallacy of aggregation.

> Entrepreneurs will endeavor to *fix the amount of employment* at the level they expect to maximize profits. (25)

Translation: employers are the cause of unemployment.
Keynes is making two separate statements here:

a. that entrepreneurs (yes, all of them, millions and millions of them) somehow collude to limit the number of jobs available, and
b. that there is such thing as an amount of employment.

The impossibility of the first assertion should be obvious to any observer.

The second statement is of far greater consequence. It links with several statements Keynes made about the *total amount of employment*.

The *total amount of employment*, also known as the *lump of labor fallacy* is a strange concept which can be summed up as follows: there are as many jobs as there are, and there will never be any new ones, so it is the job of the economist to distribute them. Also, entrepreneurs are not the creators of employment but criminals conspiring against humankind and should be placed under the direct control of an economist——if allowed to exist at all.

3. And then some more:

> The volume of employment is fixed by the entrepreneur under the motive of seeking to maximize his present and prospective profits. The volume of employment depends on the aggregate demand function.
>
> Expressed differently the expectation of an increased excess of investment over saving will induce entrepreneurs to increase the volume of employment and output. (77-78)

Translation: inflation creates jobs.

The first section of this quotation is a repetition and expansion of the previous point: "the volume of employment is fixed by the entrepreneur" (who this monster is and how he achieves his deviant aims we are not told). Keynes then uses the opportunity to introduce a demonstrably false statement: "the volume of employment depends on the aggregate demand function." (It is actually a function of the supply of labor by workers and potential workers and the demand thereof by employers and not some fantastical "aggregate demand.")

The last part is a not-so-surreptitious attempt to establish in the mind of the reader that inflation—that is, the loss of purchasing power of the cash held by the population—will induce employers to hire. Absolutely nothing could be further from the truth. When the purchasing power of money is falling anybody with money seeks to protect what they have, normally by stashing gold or foreign currency in safes, property, and works of art, not by hiring more people. We have seen this all over the world since 2007.

4. Now we are ready for some wholesale destruction of the Western way of life.

> The above (a convoluted and patently false statement, the reader should explore at his leisure, or –preferably- not at all) is closely analogous with the proposition which harmonizes the liberty which every individual possesses to change whenever he chooses the amount of money he holds with the necessity for the total amount of money which individual balances add up to be exactly equal to the amount of cash which the banking system has created. (84)

Translation: if you don't spend your money, the government will spend it for you.

This is pretty complicated stuff, but understanding it is of such fundamental importance that I beg the reader to bear with me for a few paragraphs.

There is more to money than the eye can see, or rather there is *more money* than the eye can see. Why? On top of whatever amount of physical currency there happens to be at any point, every time someone takes a nickel to the bank and it is subsequently lent, new money has entered the system.

What?

Let me give you an example: if you take one hundred dollars to the bank to deposit in your account you "have" one hundred dollars. Really, the bank owes you one hundred dollars.

Now, the bank lends eighty dollars to Mr. Jones to buy a new coffee machine for his coffee shop. He promises to repay the eighty dollars over a six-month period. He leaves the bank with eighty dollars, while you still "have" your one hundred dollars. The bank owes you one hundred dollars, while Mr. Jones owes the bank eighty dollars.

Mr. Jones buys his machine, and the vendor deposits his eighty dollars in his bank account. The bank owes you one hundred dollars and owes the coffee machine vendor eighty dollars, while Mr. Jones owes the bank eighty dollars.

Out of the new eighty-dollar deposit, the bank lends sixty dollars to Ms. Harris, who needs a new laptop. She leaves the bank with her sixty dollars, and now you have one hundred dollars, the coffee machine vendor has eighty, and Ms. Harris has sixty. What started as one hundred dollars is now one hundred plus eighty plus sixty. Magic? Not quite. Apart from you, all these people will have to return the money by either providing services to the public (as in the case of the coffee shop owner) or by paying out of future paychecks (as in the case of Ms. Harris, who happens to be a lawyer).

The amount of money is thus made by whatever the public (in this case you) owned outright and the money the banking system has created and which needs to be repaid.

This process of money creation by the banking system, which would go on ad infinitum if uninterrupted, is rarely inflationary (that is, it rarely leads to widespread increase in prices). That's because borrowers have to produce new goods or services or simply refrain from purchasing other things to repay it. The *new money* is chasing *new goods and services*, not bidding up the ones that were there before (as is the case when governments simply print fresh cash and give it away as handouts, so-called quantitative easing).

You may have by now realized that when people are happy and all is good in the world, this process of money creation by the banking system accelerates as people demand loans to buy things in the belief that they will be able to repay. Meanwhile businesses expand in expectation of even better times ahead or simply to satisfy the desires of their customers, who by virtue of feeling confident about the future indulge in a few extra things they would not pursue in more subdued times.

But unbeknown to Keynes, confidence is the result of governments living within their means. Why? Because governments that live within their means will do what they promise to do and will refrain from doing what they promise not to do. Governments in distress are base and brutal beggars who don't take no for an answer and who forget all promises in the process of saving themselves.

Now back to the theory. What Keynes is telling us is pretty simple: if people suddenly feel like not spending, it is the government's role to spend their money for them by taxing the money away, by borrowing it, or by simply debasing it via the printing presses of the central bank—usually by all three at the same time.

What's wrong with all this? There is a long and a short answer to this question. The long answer is "everything."

Why?

- At no point does the policymaker ask why if businesses love to grow and consumers love to consume, they suddenly stopped doing it. (Excessive taxation? Excessive regulation? Anti-business political rhetoric? A sudden shock?) Maybe the citizens of the country know something the government official doesn't know. In the Keynesian mind, the idea that the accumulated knowledge of humankind could be larger than the knowledge of one single government official is inconceivable.

- As people repay their debts (effectively taking out of circulation the amount of cash the banking system has created) to keep the total amount of cash constant (that is, to replace all the cash the banking system has created and that no longer exists) requires printing money on a large scale and giving it away to all and sundry in the hope that once the process of money creation by the banking system gains momentum (a return of confidence), it can be taken out of circulation, thus preventing any inflationary spiral.

  This is, needless to say, absolute nonsense. As private decision makers (that is, you and me) see the government gambling the house away, the last thing on their mind would be to invest or to hire new personnel.

- Finally, to use a medical analogy, keeping the total amount of money constant after a collapse in confidence is akin to artificially keeping the blood pressure of a patient that has just suffered a heart attack at the peak level before the attack. Even if one succeeded in doing it, one by one all the organs would shut down.

The reader may have noticed that Professor Milton Friedman is hardly mentioned in this book. Though I wholeheartedly admire Professor Friedman, he not only agreed with Keynes on the point above, but went on to "prove" that the Great Depression was the result of the Federal Reserve's failure to keep the total amount of money constant.

Professor Friedman did not live to see QE I, QE II, QE III, and their successors. If he had, he would have learned that the best monetary policy (and this is a pretty bad one) is no match for an ideologically motivated government committed to the destruction of the country's economy for ideological reasons.

Suffice here to quote Professor Hayek's damning indictment on his friend:

He was a macroeconomist.

Here's an example: After the spectacular collapse of a government-sponsored credit boom during the 1980s, the government of Japan has wholeheartedly embraced Keynes's and Friedman's ideas regarding monetary policy after a slump. Instead of analyzing the causes of the slump —exorbitant taxation, runaway government spending, political manipulation of the banking system, restrictive regulation of internal commerce, among many others— and acting on them, the government has embarked in a senseless borrowing, taxing, and spending spree.

The result has been nothing short of a global catastrophe: the more the government wasted money on bridges to nowhere, the more the business community and the public at large lost confidence in the future. Now Japan is mired in a two-decade long slump and creaks under a mountain of debt, while living standards continue to deteriorate.

Spending like there is no tomorrow only guarantees that there will be no tomorrow.

5.Waste is wealth; wealth is waste.

> Public works, even of doubtful utility may pay for themselves over and over again at a time of severe unemployment, if only from the diminished cost of relief expenditure. (127)
> Pyramid building, earthquakes and even wars may serve to increase wealth. (129)

One doesn't know whether to laugh or to cry after reading this. Building pyramids may be good for tourism five thousand years after the event. As to exactly how a person who has died as a result of a natural disaster is wealthier than when he was alive I remain puzzled.

It is worth remembering that Keynes wrote this as the world prepared for World War II in which an estimated fifty million people lost their lives and did not become wealthier as a result.

But these are logical objections, and Keynes was impervious to logic as was Marx before him and their followers today.

What about the argument that wealth would be increased *"if only from the diminished cost of relief expenditure"*? The objections to this statement are, as we shall see, insurmountable.

Building even the most trivial structures using unemployed people, who may have no building skills whatsoever, is bound to cost significantly more than paying relief.

- Building or producing things nobody wants or needs does not have a knock-on effect on wealth creation. After building a bridge to nowhere, there is not going to be a single extra loaf of bread or an extra pound of sugar on any table.
- Vast government projects are unlikely to be tailor-made for the skills of the unemployed, who may come from all walks of life.
- If a particular industry has entered terminal decline, workers previously employed in that industry would be wasting the time they should be using in retraining for real, viable, productive jobs.
- Any project commissioned by a government will have to draw managerial and project management skills (which are rarely if ever unemployed) from profitable, viable undertakings, destroying wealth, creating shortages, and increasing the price of specialized labor.
- From a practical point of view, by the time the government got its act together and launched the project, the economy would have turned the corner and the extra spending would only add to inflation— assuming that the recession is not being deliberately continued by political design.

6. Stability is chaos; chaos is stability.

The expectation of a fall in the value of money stimulates investment and employment generally. (141)

Translation: Inflation and the expectation of inflation increase employment.

Again, nothing could be further from the truth. The expectation of a fall in the value of money leads people to protect themselves by either buying foreign currencies that are not expected to be debased (or at least not sharply) or buying gold or shares or property or whatever they can lay their hands on. What they would never do in such circumstances is expand business and hire new people.

Keynes's ability to continue to harm the world economy beyond the grave does not detract from the fact that harm is all you'll ever get from this man. Sound management of public finances and sound currency (together with the protection of property and the enforcement of contracts) remain the pillars of prosperity the world over. Why? Because they allow wealth creators (employers, employees, and the self-employed) to concentrate on creating wealth instead of panicking about inflation, soaring interest rates, credit crunches, or runaway taxation.

7. Poverty is wealth; wealth is poverty.

> Of the maxims of orthodox finance none, surely, is more antisocial than the fetish of liquidity, the doctrine that it is a positive virtue on the part of investment institutions to concentrate their resources upon the holding of "liquid" securities. (155)

Translation: banks and corporations should remain illiquid; every liquidity crisis that follows is just a useful excuse for more money to be printed and given away. Here Keynes uses the word *orthodox* to elicit a negative reaction. Yet the alternative to *orthodox finance* is obviously *bankruptcy*.

But this point is crucial in another, more subtle respect: we are told that sound financial management is not only bad business, but is also inimical to society as a whole. This is the expansion of "what's good for each one of us is bad for all of us" to encompass the corporate world and, of course, government.

In other words, if living your life in a productive and orderly manner is bad for society, because a society made up of people who live productive and orderly lives is a failed society, it only follows that running corporations in a productive and orderly manner is bad for society, as bankrupt companies are the best way to ensure societal success. Needless to say, running the state and the currency on sound, prudential basis can only be bad for the country.

Here's an example: When the recent credit crunch hit the world, well-run companies stood on their own two feet. Banks that failed to ensure liquidity had to be rescued by taxpayers everywhere. To do so, governments printed trillions and gave them away, which is exactly what Keynes had in mind. He knew that, according to Lenin, there is no surer way to destroy a society than to debauch its currency.

8. To be free is to do as you are told, or else.

> I expect to see the State, which is in a position to calculate the marginal efficiency of capital-goods on long views and on the basis of general social advantage, taking an ever greater responsibility for directly organizing investment. (164)

Translation: governments should direct investment with the sole purpose of keeping people employed, regardless of the quality, quantity, or desirability of the output. "General social advantage" invariably means the electoral advantage of the man in charge of the checkbook. The social advantage could never be general, neither in a democracy nor in a dictatorship, since the officials in charge can only take from some (usually whoever does not vote for them) and give to others (usually whoever supports them).

Ever greater responsibility means until all decision making, even to the minutest level, is in the hands of a government official, preferably an economist.

On this point Keynes shows himself to be far more of a Marxist than Karl Marx ever was.

9. Slavery is freedom; freedom is slavery.

> To suppose that a flexible wage policy is a right and proper adjunct of a system which on the whole is one of laissez faire, is the opposite of the truth. (269)

Translation: government —or union— enforced, above-market salaries do not cause unemployment; they are just another useful excuse for printing money and giving it away. (After a short period of government-enforced above-market salaries, governments have no alternative but to enforce below-market salaries violently to avoid total meltdown.)

The freedom to sell or to withhold one's services is the basis of a free society (the opposite is, of course, slavery). The freedom to sell one's services includes the freedom to sell them to whomever I want at the best price I can get. Denying this is the opposite of the truth.

10. Peace is war; war is peace.

> The mercantilists were under no illusions as to the nationalistic character of their policies and their tendency to promote war. Intellectually their realism is much preferable to the confused thinking of contemporary advocates of laissez faire in international lending. (348)

Translation: workers should do as the economists dictate (in what they do, how much they earn in return and what they spend it on), or they shall die in the battlefield. No alternative (such as wage flexibility, self-employment, foreign investment, migration, or retraining) should be considered, fostered, or tolerated. Anyone who disagrees should be treated with scorn by the economists.

As we have seen on the ten points above (and will see in the section below), the *General Theory* is neither general nor a theory, as it applies only to the 1930s and is an extremely detailed national-socialist program.

It is not surprising that the first person to congratulate Keynes after the publication of *The General Theory in 1936* was the leader of the British Fascists (who congratulated him on his conversion to their cause—something Keynes vehemently denied).

KEYNES'S TWENTY-FOUR POISON PILLS

I called this section "twenty-four poison pills" simply because the *General Theory* is composed of twenty-four chapters. There are a lot more than twenty-four poison pills in the book, but listing them all would be both tiresome and dismaying. So I have selected one per chapter— no more.

The whole book is designed to turn the uninitiated into a sincere and committed enemy of liberty, prosperity, and the rule of law, of course for the purpose of protecting liberty (which is slavery), prosperity (which is poverty), and the rule of law (which is unlimited, arbitrary government power).

1. Book 1. Chapter 1. The General Theory

> I shall argue that the postulates of the classical theory[6*] are applicable to a special case only. Its teaching is misleading and disastrous if we attempt to apply it to the facts of experience. (3)

If communism was to triumph in the long run, then liberty, prosperity, and the rule of law had to be made repugnant (or at least deemed unrealistic desires or unsustainable realities) to the intellect of the leading classes—that is, the professional politicians, the media stars, the academics, the economists, and the civil servants.

2. Book 1. Chapter 2. The Postulates of the Classical Economists

Where to start? Chapter two is an inexhaustible source of poison. The reader is well advised to read it in all its gory glory. I believe it can be summed up in this passage:

> With a given organization, equipment and technique, real wages and the volume of output (and hence of employment) are uniquely correlated, so that in general, an increase in employment can only occur to the accompaniment of a decline in the rate of real wages. (17)

We are here fully introduced to the outline of the Keynesian world: entrepreneurship, technological advance, advances in productivity, new products and services, and new export markets are figments of the imagination. The only way to increase employment is to print money and give it away.

We are again reintroduced to the other pillar: the lump of labor fallacy, which holds that there is only so much work to go around and that the role of the state is to force its redistribution against the will of workers and employers alike (for the benefit of workers and employers, of course).

6* "Classical economists" was a term coined by Marx to encompass all thinkers in the field of economics before Marx. Keynes uses the term to encompass all economic thinkers before Keynes. Keynes tacitly includes Marx among the "classical economists," since he never challenged his predecessors. The reason is simple: Marx saw no need to *deny* reality in order to *change* it. Keynes also wanted to effect change but intuitively realized that for the victims of Marxism, liberty, prosperity, and the rule of law remained desirable features of life, even if they only lived in people's memories.

For example, printing money to keep nonviable businesses from folding; creating millions of government nonjobs; early retirement programs for perfectly productive workers; and wholesale granting of disability benefits on dubious medical evidence all follow from the desire to have more people collecting a salary but chasing *the same goods and services*: "a decline in the rate of real wages"

3. Book 1. Chapter 3. The Principle of Effective Demand

> Malthus[7*] indeed had vehemently opposed Ricardo's doctrine that it was impossible for effective demand to be deficient. But vainly. (32)

Here Keynes introduces us to a most bizarre concept: it is not the role of the entrepreneur to tempt consumers with her goods and services, but the role of the consumer to go and buy whatever is offered to him whether he wants it or not. The absurdity of this proposition pales in comparison with its implications: it is the government role to either force people to consume whatever businesses want to sell from time to time or to create consumers out of thin air by paying people to perform some kind of nonjob.

The result is ever-decreasing output, ever-decreasing purchasing power and ever-increasing alienation (most people hate turning up to waste a full day, even if they are paid a few pennies to do so), and social decay. In other words, the result is poverty (which is wealth) and death (which is life).

4. Book 2. Chapter 4. The Choice of Units

In chapter four, Keynes rambles along, confusing himself to the point of agreeing with what he tried to disprove and then glossing over the fact. There are several poisonous stings throughout this chapter; the most deadly is probably the easiest to miss:

> On *every* particular occasion, …an entrepreneur is concerned with decisions as to the scale on which to work a given capital equipment;

[7*] Malthius was a priest turned economist who predicted the impending doom of humankind by starvation in 1798 and was singlehandedly responsible for instigating what can only be described as the first comprehensive attempt to breed the poor out of existence (through hunger and ill treatment) for their own good, as always, both in Britain and the Commonwealth.

and when we say that the expectation of an increased demand, i.e. a raising of the aggregate demand function, will lead to an increase in aggregate output, we really mean that the firms, which own the capital equipment, will be induced to associate with it a greater aggregate employment of labor. (40, emphasis his)

Did you miss it?

If on *every* particular occasion entrepreneurs face short-term decisions, it follows that they *never* face long-term decisions (such as capital investments, staying or leaving an industry or specific line within the industry, and so on). In his pedantic incoherence, Keynes is telling us that there is no such thing as long-term planning, but only a collection of short-term planning incidents.

If government policymakers manage to give inflationary jolts to demand on a regular basis, given the existing capital equipment (no decision to add or to subtract to it is even admitted as a possibility in the Keynesian world), employment will be kept at perpetually high or even increasing levels. The running to the ground of all or substantially all the industrial capabilities of Britain and America between 1945 and 1985 is testament to this policy. Modern Detroit, where we can see grass growing where auto plants once employed hundreds of thousands is another painful reminder of just how much harm bad economic policies can inflict on an unsuspecting population.

5. Book 2. Chapter 5. Expectation as Determining Output and Employment

This chapter is more revealing for what it does not contain than for what it does: the decision to mothball industrial capacity, to transfer it overseas, or to stop production altogether. What we *are* told is no less misleading:

> Now, in general, a change in expectations (whether short-term or long-term) will only produce its full effect on employment over a considerable period.... In the case of short term expectations this is because changes in expectations are not, as a rule, sufficiently violent or rapid, when they are for the worse, whilst they are for the better. (47)

As usual with Keynes's statements, nothing could be further from the truth: when people panic, their reaction is instant. When they start to feel more comfortable, they often take a long time to act on their newfound enthusiasm.

This passage has led policymakers to underestimate the extent and speed with which their attacks on industry, trade, and finance translate into diminished output and employment.

6. Book 2. Chapter 6. The Definition of Income, Saving and Investment

To convince the reader that poverty is wealth and that wealth is poverty, Keynes has to slowly confuse the reader as to the nature of his argument. Thus, by redefining income as expenditure, saving as unnecessary and counterproductive antisocial behavior, and investment as spending, in chapter six he lays the foundation of this philosophy.

> Common sense and the great majority of the economists tell us that:
>> Income = value of output = consumption + investment
>> Saving = income – consumption
>> Saving = investment
>
> ...It is only by denying the validity of one or other of them that the conclusion can be avoided.
>
> ...Hence, in the aggregate the excess of income over consumption, which we call, saving, cannot differ from the addition to capital equipment which we call investment.
>
> The decision to consume and the decisions to invest between them determine incomes.
>
> Assuming that the decisions to invest become effective, they must in doing so either curtail consumption or expand income.
>
> Thus the act of investment in itself cannot help causing saving to increase by a corresponding amount. (63)

Confused?

Keynes finds himself in an untenable position: if savings are antisocial, where is investment going to come from? (Let's remember that his economic philosophy calls for running to the ground all existing legacy investment, not for adding to their stock.) His solution is to claim that investment (which obviously appears out of thin air) that is the *cause* of savings.

Still confused?

If only we can make investment happen, while everyone is consuming every penny or unit of output produced, then savings will grow *deus ex machina* as a result of the investment.

As the recent crisis hit, many governments around the world decided to "spend their way back to prosperity". All they got was more debt and no prosperity. Their —rather absurd— confusion stems directly out of Chapter 6 of the General Theory.

7. Book 2. Chapter 7. The Meaning of Saving and Investment Further Considered

This is the vital difference between the theory of the economic behaviors of the aggregate and the theory of the behavior of the individual unit, in which we assume that changes in the individual's own demand do not affect his income. (85)

This is more of the same: only by running his own finances to the ground can an individual ensure that his income remains high. The absurdity of this proposition needs little explanation. A society of bankrupt households (and companies, local authorities, and central government) can hardly be said to be prosperous, and a society where savings and investments are made impossible would never be able to innovate or to expand production to provide for and to employ the rising generation.

Running the economy to the ground makes sense only if we all die at the same time as the capital equipment ceases to be operational.

8. Book 3. Chapter 8. The Propensity to Consume. 1. The Objective Factors

The obstacle to a clear understanding is much the same as in many academic discussions on capital, namely, an inadequate appreciation of the fact that capital is not a self-subsistent entity existing apart from consumption. On the contrary, every weakening in the propensity to consume regarded as a permanent habit must weaken the demand for capital as well as the demand for consumption. (106)

Here Keynes is particularly perverse: by equating capital and demand for capital—presumably within one country—he convinces the reader that the more a society prepares the terrain for a more prosperous future (by saving more of its income or part of some suddenly increased income), the poorer they become.

Again, exactly the opposite is true: as capital becomes more abundant and therefore cheaper, more and more commercial and social undertakings that did not make sense at the time of greater scarcity suddenly begin to make sense. Here are three examples: building a primitive power station on limited resources and then replacing it with a state-of-the-art, less-polluting one; Moving from a basic transport infrastructure to high-tech infrastructure; and building basic housing and slowly moving to high-quality housing as capital accumulates.

Alternatively an aging population would choose to invest part of its savings in promising developing countries with younger populations. For example, as the people of Japan began to prepare for the demographic winter, the Keynesian bureaucracy and political class decided to keep the country spending as if it were a young country with a long and exciting future ahead of it. The result has been 220 percent debt-to-GDP ratio and an economy in permanent slump.

Adam Smith had answered this nonsense 160 years earlier:

> The demand for labor increases with the increase of stock whatever be its profits; and after these are diminished, stock may not only continue to increase, but to increase much faster than before. …A great stock, though with small profits, generally increases faster than a small stock with great profits.
> The increase of stock, which raises wages, tends to lower profit.

9. Book 3. Chapter 9. The Propensity to Consume. 2. The Subjective Factors

In chapter nine, Keynes spectacularly fails to convince anyone that depriving the monetary authority of any means to ensure a stable currency and low inflation is the best way to ensure growth. However, he continues undeterred:

> The more virtuous we are the more determinedly thrifty the more obstinately orthodox in our national and personal finance, the more our incomes will have to fall. (111)

He goes on to qualify this statement with this condition: "when interest rises relatively to the marginal efficiency of capital." But "marginal efficiency of capital" is a meaningless concoction of the Keynesian mind, which will have to be determined by government, based on so-called long-term social advantages. Make no mistake; he is calling for the destruction of the currency, no holds barred, which is the almost exclusive aim of his ramblings.

10. Book 3. Chapter 10. The Marginal Propensity to Consume and the Multiplier

Chapter ten is quite fun to read, as Keynes displays a novice's ignorance of accounting conventions. But most importantly, we are introduced to the Keynesian multiplier, which basically holds that for every dollar the government wastes, the economy returns about a dollar and a half of economic output.

By Keynes's own admission, the Keynesian multiplier should have been called the Kahnsian multiplier, as it was the brainchild of Richard Ferdinand (later Baron) Kahn. The fact that the Keynesian or Kahnsian multiplier is just a figment of the good baron's imagination is less relevant than the thought process used to explain as a fact something that has never before or since been shown to be true in reality. It goes like this:

> The multiplier tells us by how much their employment has to be increased to yield an increase in real income sufficient to induce them to do the *necessary* extra saving (which was antisocial, remember?) and is a function of their psychological propensities. (117)

The "multiplier" tells us how much the cart needs to pull the horses before the horses grow wings, fly away, and decide to nest and lay their eggs at the bottom of the ocean.

11. Book 4. Chapter 11. The Marginal Efficiency of Capital

For anyone with a vested interest in retaining their sanity, it is better not to venture into chapter eleven and Keynes's discussion of "the marginal efficiency of capital," which he defines as

> being equal to that rate of discount which would make the present value of the series of annuities given by the returns expected from the capital-asset during its life equal to its supply price [which he defines elsewhere as the "direct cost," which he calls "replacement cost"]. (135)

Please let me translate it for you: Government should have the increasingly exclusive right to direct investment, which should in turn come from thin air—or more precisely the printing presses of the central bank—and never from savings, unless those savings are the result of spending, which by definition they cannot be.

If the government can be bothered to justify its actions at all, every new investment should be justified by a number, called the "marginal efficiency of capital," which is simultaneously meaningless and incomprehensible, impossible to prove or disprove, and can be quickly and easily made up for the occasion. Investment, if any, will be directed to politically profitable endeavors.

12. Book 4. Chapter 12. The State of Long Term Expectation

In this chapter we are told that, despite Keynes's contention that "in the long run we are all dead," it is very important to take the long run into consideration. The conclusion of the chapter is, as we saw in point eight, the main tenet of Keynesianism: the government is uniquely positioned to direct investment.

However, the real poison pill comes a few pages earlier: After arguing that *liquid and efficient capital markets are a bad thing* for the economy, he tells us:

> The introduction of a substantial Government transfer tax (financial transaction tax, Tobin tax, stamp duty, etc.) on all transactions might prove the most serviceable reform available, with a view to mitigating the predominance of speculation over enterprise in the United States. (160)

If the highest standard of living in history for the largest number of people in history for the longest period in history all combined with the greatest degree of liberty in history were the result of "speculation over enterprise in the United States," it would be the greatest endorsement ever for speculation over enterprise.

This is, of course, absolute nonsense—just like the rest of the *General Theory*.

13. Book 4. Chapter 13. The General Theory of the Rate of Interest

In chapter ten we learn that Keynes did not understand accounting. In chapter thirteen we learn that he also failed to grasp the concept of money. We are told,

> Just as we found that the marginal efficiency of capital is fixed, not by the "best" opinion, but by the market valuation as determined by mass psychology, so also expectations as to the future of the rate of interest as fixed by mass psychology, have their reactions on liquidity preference;

but with this addition that the individual, who believes that future rates of interest will be above the rates assumed by the market has a reason for keeping actual liquid cash whilst the individual who differs from the market in the other direction will have a motive for borrowing money for short periods in order to purchase debts of longer term. The market price will be fixed at the point at which the sales of the "bears" and the purchases of the "bulls" are balanced. (170)

I am not making this up. I promise. But he continues,

Thus every increase in the quantity of money must raise the price of bonds sufficiently to exceed the expectations of some "bull" and so influence him to sell his bond for cash and join the "bear" brigade. (171)

And then he goes in for the kill:

If however there is negligible demand for the cash from the speculative motive except for a *short transitional interval*, an increase in the quantity of money will have to lower the rate of interest almost forthwith, in whatever degree is necessary to raise employment and the wage-unit sufficiently to cause the additional cash to be absorbed by the transactions-motive and the precautionary motive. (171)

Just in case you missed it, here it is: if the entire population is on the brink of starvation and the corporate world is starved of capital, any newly printed or borrowed cash the government puts into circulation will be instantly put to work in satisfying basic, unsatisfied needs by using additional workers.

Why didn't anyone think of it before, one wonders. Maybe because three-hundred-yard-long lines in front of empty shops in communist Russia never motivated anyone to bake an extra loaf of bread. Or maybe because after the entire financial architecture of the country is dismantled (thereby starving consumers of the means to consume and entrepreneurs of the means to invest), any addition to the money supply triggers an increase in prices, not extra work—and most definitely not extra output.

14. Book 4. Chapter 14. The Classical Theory of the Rate of Interest

In trying to disprove the theory of the rate of interest, which he qualifies as the "classical" theory of the rate of interest, Thoroughly Modern Maynard introduces what is probably the only true statement in the whole book. But then he tries to disprove it.

> The rate of interest is the factor which brings the demand for investment and the willingness to save into equilibrium with one another. (175)

He fails to disprove the above but doesn't miss the opportunity to peddle cart pulling the horses arguments that investment comes before savings.

> Now the analysis of the previous chapters will have made it plain that this account of the matter (the "classical" theory) must be erroneous. The traditional analysis has been aware that saving depends on income but it has overlooked the fact that income depends on investment, in such fashion that, when investment changes, income must necessarily change in just that degree which is necessary to make the change in saving equal to the change in investment. (177)

This means that since investment is the result of consumption, savings are the result of no consumption, it follows that *savings are an impediment to investment*. Policymakers should deter savings by whatever means possible, especially through rampant inflation and by keeping the public from accessing any type of investment that could shield them from its harmful effects (through a "government transfer tax").

15. Book 4. Chapter 15. The Psychological and Business Incentives to Liquidity

In chapter fifteen, Keynes begins to introduce his readers to one of his most bizarre ideas: that inflation (a broad-based and sustained increase in prices) comes in two varieties: (1) increases in prices due to more people being employed and paid to produce the same amount of output, and (2) people being paid more for the same amount of output, or what he calls "true inflation," which can occur only when everybody is employed (which is never).

> It is evident, then, that the rate of interest is a *highly psychological* phenomenon. (202)
> It might be more accurate, perhaps, to say that the rate of interest is a *highly conventional,* rather than a highly psychological, phenomenon. (203)

Confused?

> The great fault in the quantity theory is that it does not distinguish between changes in prices which are a function of changes in output,[8*] and those which are a function of the changes in the wage-unit. The explanation of this omission is, perhaps, to be found in the assumptions that there is no propensity to hoard (save) and that there is always full employment. (209)

Here Keynes simultaneously introduces the ideas that inflation is not inflation but something altogether different from inflation and that it can be either created by paying people to do nothing (in which case it is not inflation) or by paying people more money to do the same amount of work as before, which of course is not inflation unless everybody is employed (again, which is never). Or, he says, inflation can be "real" when it is created by paying more to people to do the same when everybody is employed, which never happens, (He expands this concept in chapter twenty-one.)

To cut a long story short, there is no such thing as inflation, and if you see prices going through the roof, you are clearly delusional.

16. Book 4. Chapter 16. Sundry Observations on the Nature of Capital

By chapter sixteen, Keynes feels bold enough to make a frontal attack on capitalism, as such: the foundations of capitalism (liberty and the rule of law) and the outcome of capitalism (prosperity).

The reader can be left in no doubt as to what Keynes intentions are. We are told that savings are always and everywhere a bad thing:

8* Remember that Keynes defines changes in output as those additions *to the workforce* that are expected to add neither to the production of goods nor to the provision of services—that is, the creation of nonjobs paid for by diluting the value of the existing stock of money, via the printing presses of the central bank. By changes in output he means no changes in output.

> It is not a substitution of future consumption-demand for present consumption-demand, it is a net diminution of such demand...which depresses prices and the marginal efficiency of existing capital. (210)

That's the whole point of saving and investing: to have more things that can *make* more things with less effort. That's what makes (or used to make) the life of every generation better than that of the previous one.

> Since the expectation of consumption is the only raison d'être of employment, there should be nothing paradoxical in the conclusion that a diminished propensity to consume has a depressing effect on employment. (211)

Next time your employer threatens to fire you for doing a lousy job, just remind her that she employs you only so that you can consume and that if you stop consuming, she is out of business. Wait to see the reaction.

According to Keynes, businesses conspire against the community:

> Capital has to be kept scarce enough in the long-period to have a marginal efficiency which is at least equal to the rate of interest for a period equal to the life of the capital. (217)

But despair not. The economist comes to the rescue:

> *If I am right* in supposing it to be comparatively easy to make capital-goods so abundant that the marginal efficiency of capital is zero, this may be the most sensible way of gradually getting rid of many of the objectionable features of capitalism. (221)

But he is *not* right.

Kill the pensioners, present and future:

> For a little reflection will show what enormous social changes would result from a gradual disappearance of a rate of return on accumulated wealth. (221)

We are already seeing the "enormous social changes" that low-interest-rate policies of counterfeiting the currency are having: the elderly are suffering.

But, hey, the economy is booming. But wait. Both the elderly and the young (and everyone in between) are hurting while the economy stagnates and prices rise.

Look on the bright side: economists are in great demand.

17. Book 4. Chapter 17. The Essential Properties of Interest and Money

> The rate which we might term the neutral rate of interest, namely, … which is consistent with full employment given the other parameters of the system. …This rate may be better described as the optimum rate of interest. (243)

The only way to have full employment with no savings or investments is to return to a hunter-gatherer way of life: every man for himself, working from dawn to dusk, barely scraping a living. The thousands of scavengers that roam the rubbish dumps in the Keynesian paradises of the Third World may have had something to say about Keynes's optimum rate of interest.

18. Book 4. Chapter 18. The General Theory of Employment Restated

As to why Keynes feels the need to restate his *General Theory*, I remain puzzled. In chapter eighteen, we are told that we were doing fine, but we should not believe we couldn't change (what was fine). He gives no reason as to why anyone may want to change what is fine.

> The outstanding features of our actual experience; -namely, that we oscillate, in avoiding the gravest extremes of fluctuation in employment and in prices in both directions, round an intermediate position appreciably below full employment and appreciably above the minimum employment a decline below which would endanger life.
> But we must not conclude that the mean position thus determined by natural tendencies are likely to persist, failing measures expressly designed to correct them, is, therefore, established by laws of necessity or … are a principle which cannot be changed. (254)

This is not so much a poison pill as an admission that the *General Theory* is really a poor attempt to explain the Great Depression through platitudes.

Otherwise, why would anyone want to change a system that provides both prosperity and stability?

19. Book 5. Chapter 19. Changes in Money Wages

In chapter nineteen, Keynes quickly moves from his contention that it is better to debase the currency than to allow employers and employees to reach new and satisfactory agreements within the framework of a healthy currency. Not satisfied in recommending the debasement of the currency to accommodate unaffordable compensation arrangements each and every time a trade union oversteps the mark, he gives a dire and totally unfounded warning that if at any point the government abandons its inflationary policies, kittens will die and angels will lose their feathers.

> It follows that if labor were to respond to conditions of gradually diminishing employment by offering its services at a gradually diminishing money wage, this would not, as a rule, have the effect of reducing real wages[9*] and might even have the effect of increasing them.... The chief result of this policy would be to cause a great instability of prices, so violent perhaps as to make business calculations futile. (269)

So he is right. As employers and employees regularly renegotiate pay and conditions to adapt to changes, unemployment stays low and wages grow in terms of purchasing power (although not necessarily in terms of money) more often than not. But the threat of "great instability in prices, so violent..." has no basis, neither in theory nor in economic history.

This irrational fear of deflation keeps Western central banks constantly debasing their currencies for no reason at all, causing financial mishaps and misallocations of credit, which are always blamed on capitalism. The well informed

---

[9*] Reducing real wages to increase—or more precisely, to redistribute employment—as the best or rather the only way to increase total employment is a feature of Keynesian policymaking, and it is based as we have already seen on the lump of labor fallacy. A real economist cares about overall employment *and* quality of life, not just about keeping people entertained while they do nothing.

and the well-connected enjoy a risk-free arbitrage by which they make billions at everyone else's expense.

20. Book 5. Chapter 20. The Employment Function

> There is, perhaps, something a little perplexing in the apparent asymmetry between inflation and deflation. For whilst a deflation of effective demand below the level required for full employment will diminish employment as well as prices, an inflation of it above this level will merely affect prices. (291)

Apart from the obvious fact that a decrease in money wages implies neither a reduction in real wages (although this is likely) nor a decrease in the level of employment (exactly the opposite being true), it is demonstrably false both in theory and in practice that inflation is as harmless as Keynes would have us believe—that is, it "*merely* affects prices." "Deflation of effective demand" is another meaningless expression created for the occasion.

Persistent inflation re-prices everything (goods, services, commodities, investments, productive assets, and the cost of finance) and changes all calculations. Inflation deters savings and tends to channel investments towards assets designed to preserve existing wealth not to create new wealth.

Of course one always must remember that in the Keynesian world *savings are antisocial and investment is contemptible.*

21. Book 5. Chapter 21. The Theory of Prices

> We cannot get rid of money even by abolishing gold and silver and legal tender instruments. So long as there exists any durable asset, it is capable of possessing monetary attributes and, therefore, of giving rise to the characteristic problems of a monetary economy. (294)

The combination of a sound banking and monetary systems is the foundation of any successful economy. The absence of a sound banking and monetary system is incompatible with liberty, since any alternative to modern monetary and banking arrangements would never produce enough cash to prevent many or even most workers from falling into slavery (I mean literal slavery), because such an economy could pay only in food and lodging at best, but never in cash so that for the workers could live their lives as they please.

Keynes seems to see only problems, where a true economist sees possibilities.

22. Book 6. Chapter 22. Notes on the Trade Cycle

Chapter twenty-two is a poisoned chalice, or rather a hysterical rant against the Western way of life.

> It is not easy to revive the marginal efficiency of capital, determined, as it is, by the *uncontrollable and disobedient psychology of the business world*. It is the return of confidence, to speak in the ordinary language, which is so insusceptible to control in an economy of individualistic capitalism. (317)

The image of Freddie Krueger telling his victims, "Trust me," spring to mind.

> In conditions of laissez faire the avoidance of wide fluctuations in employment may, therefore, prove impossible without a far reaching change in the psychology of investment markets such as there is no reason to expect. I conclude that the duty of *ordering the current volume of investment cannot be safely left in private hands.* (320)

This is the same man who elsewhere praised pyramid building, wars, and even earthquakes as the best economic policy. ("Ancient Egypt was doubly fortunate, and doubtless owed it fabled wealth, in that it possessed two activities, namely pyramid building as well as the search for precious metals" [131].)

We get here a glimpse of exactly what the government economists do when they have *the power to direct investment*: they waste it.

> In existing conditions where the volume of investment is unplanned and uncontrolled subject to the vagaries of the marginal efficiency of capital as determined by the private judgment of individuals ignorant or speculative…there is no means of securing a higher level of employment except by increasing consumption. (324)

I know I promised only one poison pill per chapter, but these three statements are pretty much what Keynes and Marx were all about.

In the final point, Keynes shamefully confuses the "volume of investment," which is carefully planned by entrepreneurs and strictly controlled by their financial, legal, and technical advisers, and the investors themselves, with "valuations of company shares" in the stock market, which, being a residual claim on the company's assets are bound to fluctuate significantly, largely due to the actions of the monetary authority, whose track record ranges from patchy to appalling.

Note also that "there is no means of securing a higher level of employment except by increasing consumption" only while "the volume of investment" is "determined by the private judgment." In other words, his economic policy is only a transitional policy before the full implementation of the planned economy.

Socialism is the transition to communism; Keynesianism is the transition to socialism.

The communist stage, of course, never arrives, as it would require that politicians *turned their limousines into ploughshares*, something they seem conspicuously reluctant to do.

23. Book 6. Chapter 23. Notes on Mercantilism, the Usury Laws, Stamped Money and Theories of Under Consumption

Here Keynes briefly describes a large number of theories and, as always, embraces the most destructive ones:

> It is the policy of an autonomous rate of interest, unimpeded by international preoccupations, and of a national investment program directed to an optimum level of domestic employment which is twice blessed in the sense that it helps ourselves and our neighbors at the same time. (349)

It was this particular policy on the part of the Roosevelt Administration and not the Versailles Treaty (as Keynes claimed) made World War II financially unavoidable.

24. Book 6. Chapter 24. Concluding Notes on the Social Philosophy Toward Which the General Theory Might Lead

Hell?

Keynes offers nothing new here: poverty is wealth.

> Thus our argument leads towards the conclusion that in contemporary conditions the growth of wealth, so far from being dependent on the abstinence of the rich, as it is commonly supposed is more likely to be impeded by it. (373)

As every penny we earn is redistributed to anyone with time on their hands to spend quickly, capital formation increasingly depends on raids on everyone's pocket via the printing presses of the central banks. This is a vain attempt to keep alive the very economy the economists are trying their very best to destroy.

The legacy of Keynes's mind is ever more frequent and more severe crisis.

CONCLUSION ON KEYNESIANISM

Whether Keynes "saved capitalism" by making the road to serfdom a bit longer and giving us time to react or he really believed that civil servants are in a better position to run enterprise than the entrepreneurs themselves is now a moot point. You may believe that he gave us time to revert to liberty, prosperity, and the rule of law or that he believed what he said. But in any case, his policies fail the ultimate test: they do not work.

The premises are false, the analysis is flawed, and the conclusions are absurd.

Inflation and currency manipulation simply add another layer of difficulty, uncertainty, and complication to business and family finances without resolving any problem. Government meddling in business planning is disastrous in the short term, the medium term, and the long run.

Keynes defeated all his rivals at the time because he gave the world what it wanted: the certainty that they could have their cake and eat it, give it away to charity, and save it for a rainy day. While his rivals wasted their energies explaining the suicidal nature of Keynes's ideas, the world moved on happily toward its ruin.

We can mend our ways and return to a sound, sustainable, and productive economy, but that requires the following:

- For the intellectual elite to start turning the tide away from socialism, Keynesianism, or whatever they call their collectivistic choices
- For the political leadership to take on entrenched interests, particularly in the educational and welfare monopolies, and win
- For the people to rediscover the dignity of earning a living through hard and/or smart work and of being the providers for their families and the masters of their destinies
- For the new generation to understand that true equality is the equality of dignity, not the equality of living standards
- For people to understand that envy is a character flaw, not the basis for sound policymaking
- For all of us to understand that the safety net should always remain a safety net and never be allowed to degenerate into a hammock or a lifestyle choice
- For Keynes to no longer be taught to future economists, not even as a curiosity (after all, witchcraft is not taught in medical schools)

Keynes was a product of the generation of intellectuals that gave us two world wars, the Gulag Archipelago, Auschwitz, and the Holocaust. As we have seen with socialism in all its forms, *Keynes adds a whole new set of problems without resolving any.*

Keynes famously claimed that "in the long run, we are all dead." The long run has come, and *they* are all dead. It's time for them to rest in peace and for us to move on.

During its rule of scarce one hundred years, capitalism has created more massive and more colossal productive forces than have all preceding generations together.

KARL MARX

CHAPTER 6

CAPITALISM

While communism is a system in its own right, capitalism, which is often portrayed as the alternative to communism, is not a system but a small, essential part of what Adam Smith called as the system of liberty, which includes all the elements of a free society, of which private property is one.

The enemies of freedom have very good reasons to promote this false dichotomy. By calling the system of liberty capitalism, they save themselves the embarrassment of calling communism the "system of slavery."

Before we start talking about the capitalist system, we need to briefly define *system*, *capital*, and *capitalism*.

A *system* is a set of interacting or interdependent components forming an integrated whole. These integrated wholes share some common characteristics, such as structure, recognizable behaviors, and interconnectivity among component parts. The term *system* may also refer to a set of rules that determine and/ or govern such structure or behavior.

Capital refers to wealth in the form of money or property used or accumulated in a business by a person, partnership, or corporation. Capital is used or available to use in the creation of more wealth. In turn, wealth is the abundance of goods and services at our disposal.

Capitalism is commonly defined as an economic system based on the private ownership of the means of production; distribution, and exchange, characterized by the freedom of capitalists to operate or manage their property for profit in competitive conditions.

It is quite easy to spot the first problem with the term *capitalism*: what we know as capitalism (that is, what Milton Friedman calls "competitive capitalism" as opposed to "state capitalism" or "crony capitalism") is not a system at all, however much we stretch the definition of *system*.

What are the interacting or interdependent components of the system of liberty?

- A *free people*, who are aware of their freedom and value it, and who are willing and capable of defending it. They also are likely to produce the leaders required for the task.
- A *moral system* conducive to and capable of sustaining freedom, particularly in the restraining of greed, envy, deception, murder, and the use of brute force.
- The *institutions* of a free people willing and capable of defending the life, the liberty (of thought, word, and deed), and the property of the individual.
- The social *arrangements* of a free society, specifically the enforcement of lawful contracts.

The interactions of these independent components form the system of liberty that we now call capitalist democracy, or liberal democracy. In this system, *who owns what* is only part of the story.

By identifying private property with the entire system of liberty, Karl Marx deliberately or unwittingly led millions of useful innocents to believe that their liberties and prosperity could and would be preserved once the right to own property had been abolished.

There are millions of people who —even today— believe that liberty and prosperity can be maintained once "capitalism" is gone. The human capacity for self-delusion knows no limits.

IS ANYONE REALLY FREE? DOES IT MATTER IF THEY ARE?

Few nations in history have been *free* in any sense of the word for any length of time. Even fewer have been willing to defend that freedom. It is not enough for a people to *reason* that freedom is good for them: *reason does not compel people to action*, only to further rationalization. Only people who are devoted to freedom with passion are able to retain it for any length of time.

The first task expected from institutions of a free society is that they *preserve themselves and remain true to their mission*. That is not possible if the underlying population has lost or never developed a taste for liberty, prosperity, and the rule of law.

The social arrangements of a free society are such that there is a leader who leads the society where he or she sees fit. Powerful checks and balances with the means and a vested interest in keeping this leader on a tight leash, lest he or she destroy the country in the process of leading it. In all ordinary affairs, justice is served.

The shape and form of these institutions may vary from time to time and from place to place, but the key requirements remain. People are not angels, however, and the temptation to do what is wrong or not to do what is right is ever present in the lives of those who reach positions of power. These temptations go far beyond what ordinary citizens can imagine.

Without at least some residual love of liberty, prosperity, and the rule of law—that is, a love of country and its people past, present, and future in the heart of the leaders of society—such free institutions will be lost, no matter how many or how cleverly designed the checks and balances may be.

People are free because they refuse to live under the coercion of others. The fact that they do not *depend* on others' whim for their survival makes liberty a *reality*.

- For the true liberal, who takes the free society and its institutions for granted, economic liberty is an end in itself.
- For the socialist and the Keynesian, economic liberty is the problem to be resolved
- For the conservative, economic liberty is a means to an end—the means to sustain a free society and its institutions, the means to a *life worth living*.

The battle over economic ideas of the past two centuries was drawn between the *individualistic materialism* of the true liberals and the *collectivistic materialism* of socialists, Marxists, and Keynesians: the modern liberals.

The true liberals saw, or believed they saw, liberty as an end in itself. This was an optical illusion: having denied the life of the spirit, liberty is the liberty to be base and brutal and cannot be sustained. The self-made person's love of liberty evaporates as soon as he or she has acquired a full complement of riches. The apparently inexplicable phenomenon of socialist billionaires is actually very easy to explain: having used what liberty was available to them to acquire their billions, they quickly realized they had no further use or love for liberty.

The socialist, and particularly the Marxist or the Keynesian, seeks to *use* liberty the other way around: as businesspeople use their liberty to amass great fortunes, professional politicians should use their political liberty to help themselves to those fortunes until both the fortunes and the liberty have been extinguished. And then there will be weeping and gnashing of teeth.

Both the true liberals and the modern-day liberals do away with liberty at the first opportunity: it is a means to an end, and that end is material. Liberals have some use for the rule of law, but this is only transitional, only until—in Keynes's words—"the seats of power and authority have been attained" after which point "there should be no more poetic license."

Socialists have no use for liberty beyond preparation for the takeover of the state.

Competitive capitalism is not a system: competitive capitalism is simply the way a free and prosperous people living under their own laws organize their economic life.

The actual system is the *system of liberty*, which includes the social, institutional, and legal arrangements of a free people: competitive capitalism is a small though essential part of that system. It is on the economic freedom that all our other freedoms depend.

The only *liberals* in the true sense of the word have been the conservatives. They did not pursue liberty or prosperity as ends in themselves, but only as part of a coherent system.

Our liberty is not dependent for its survival on the goodwill of our billionaires: if it were, it would have perished. Instead it is dependent on the desire and determination of the British and the American peoples to conserve the freedoms and the privileges that are their inheritance.

One may paraphrase the famous words of Karl Marx and say that a specter is haunting the modern mind, the specter of insecurity.

ROBERT NISBET

CHAPTER 7

WHERE WE ARE NOW AND WHERE WE ARE HEADING

Two armed ideologies threatened our world in the past one hundred years, and they were both comprehensively defeated: national socialism in 1945 with the surrender of Germany, Japan and Italy; and international socialism in 1991 with the disintegration of the Soviet Union. But that did not happen before we had adopted and fully implemented most of the economic and social measures that lead to a fate similar to theirs.

We are still standing because we took the slow road to self-destruction while our opponents charged full steam ahead. But we are still heading in the wrong direction; we are doing it more slowly and, for the time being, less violently.

Einstein defined *insanity* as doing the same thing over and over again and expecting different results. So we may be said to be living in the *age of insanity*.

In 1985 Russell Kirk warned us that Marx's prophesies, like the prophesies of Knox, were of the order of those what work their own fulfillment. If the conviction of the inevitability of communism prevails in the minds of people a few years longer, "the transition from liberal democracy to totalitarianism will not seem too arduous or unpleasant. It will indeed be scarcely noticed save by the 'utopians,' the 'reactionaries,' and 'similar eccentrics.'" And, he continued "centralization and political collectivism, nevertheless, are not irresistibly ordained, the fashionable current opinion among the intellectuals notwithstanding."

The apparent lack of violence in the gradual march toward socialism—rather, "the total state"—is delusory. The economic consequences of socialism, even in mild forms displayed in the early stages (we are somewhat past the early stages), are unemployment, cultural regression, social decay, economic stagnation, corruption, regulation for its own sake, and crony capitalism. It only gets worse over time.

Most of us work for a living, either for a salary or by running a business. There is a direct connection between a penny in our pocket and the part of our lives that was spent earning it.

Every government program achieves two things; first, it takes away our freedom to choose in that particular field. Second, it takes away more and more of life itself: every tax dollar they take away is hours, days, months, and years of your life sacrificed for the sake of a bureaucracy.

Western citizens are no longer killed by tens of millions in the battlefields. Instead, tens of millions of lives are wasted every year in ever-expanding bureaucracies. There has to be a better way.

The brave and wide-ranging reforms of the 1980s gave Britain and America—and to a lesser extent Western Europe—a new lease of life. This included healthy currencies, a manageable debt burden, a streamlined economy, a sound banking system, and a less violent labor movement. Welfare reforms in the 1990s, especially in the United States, have also arrested the decline that is the inevitable result of macroeconomic management. But those achievements, which were incomplete, have either been squandered or are in the process of being reversed.

The battle is for the hearts and minds; the economy is just a tool: we repaired and sharpened the tool, but we failed to move the hearts or to excite the minds. Liberty, prosperity and the rule of law can move hearts and the minds of the people only if they are made flesh. In other words, people have to *live* the benefits of liberty, *enjoy* the fruits of prosperity, and *feel safe* under the law.

- We have to feel that liberty is good for us, because we and our families and our communities ostensibly and measurably benefit from its exercise.
- We have to feel —once again- that prosperity is up for grabs and that it's all a matter of working hard and/or working smart.

- We have to see justice in action for our benefit and that of our families and communities.

But just as importantly, we need to be constantly reminded that liberty, prosperity and the rule of law are not *naturally occurring phenomena* nor can they be combined with whatever social, political, or economic arrangements.

The enemies of liberty know this all too well. Modern conservatives do not.

As we saw in Chapter 4, Marx proposed ten key measures to move from the system of liberty to a system of slavery, which he called communism. The most important ones have been in operation for at least two generations—namely, "a heavy progressive or graduated income tax" and "the centralization of credit in the hands of the state, by means of a national bank with state capital and an exclusive monopoly."

We are firmly back on the *road to serfdom* and marching apace. Whether this march is continued, accelerated, slowed down, (momentarily) stopped, or reversed will depend on the behavior of our leaders and our citizens in the incoming years.

The current generation of leaders, indoctrinated to look forward to an ever-expanding state, is not only incapable of altering this trend. In fact, they cannot even imagine why they should do such a thing. Changing course will require the very men and women our mass education system is designed to eradicate. The education system has become the most implacable enemy of diversity: we either change it or we shall perish as a free people.

We are in trouble, but the cause of liberty, prosperity, and the rule of law is not lost just yet. We just need to break the curse of the dead economists.

Some socialists seem to believe that people should *be numbers on a state computer: we believe they* should *be individuals. We are all unequal. No one, thank heavens, is quite like anyone else, however much the socialists may pretend otherwise. And we believe that everyone has the right to be unequal.*

But to us every human being is equally important: *A man's right to work as he will, To spend what he earns, To own property, To have the state as servant, and not as master,*

They are the essences of a free economy and on that freedom all our other freedoms *depend.*

MARGARET THATCHER

CHAPTER 8

THE ECONOMICS OF CONSERVATISM

Now, it is fine explain how free-market fundamentalism takes liberty and the rule of law for granted, thus failing to make provisions for their survival: society is a lot more than just a market, and countries are a lot more than the sum of the individuals who live in them.

It is fine to explain why collectivism in its mild socialist form or in its more extreme communist incarnation is the very opposite of true community and leads to corruption, stagnation, and social decay or hunger, slavery, and death, respectively: if people are not allowed to enjoy the fruits of their efforts, they will make no effort.

We can all agree that corporatism, whether in its Keynesian form or the more violent fascist or national socialist form, is a threat to our liberty, our prosperity, and the rule of law. It is almost as destructive as that of socialism; combine political and economic power in one set of hands, and any system of checks and balances becomes dead letter on a forgotten scroll. **Liberalism, collectivism, and corporatism are all remedies from the same laboratory; they cure none of the ills of a free society and instead add myriad side effects of their own making.**

Is there any alternative to all this? Is it for the conservatives to find it? Or should they simply hold the fort till progressives come up with yet another plan?

Some may even argue that the role of conservatives is to pick up the pieces, splicing the ragged ends after yet another bout of progressive mismanagement— the political version of a repairs and maintenance team.

Maybe.

The party of order and the party of progress are two aspects of a healthy society. The party of order reminds us *how much we already have*, how much effort and sacrifice were required to achieve it, and how difficult it would be to restore it once it's been lost. The party of progress ensures that new ideas, new solutions, and new approaches are given a fair chance or simply makes sure that youthful transformational energy is diverted through the channels of the Constitution, thus preempting the twin perils of social instability on the one side and social ossification (which leads to instability) on the other.

But the order has been shattered, and it needs to be restored.

The principle of envy, enshrined in the ideas of equality of living conditions or equality in general, has displaced all other beliefs. Societies tend toward stagnation, and we may simply be trapped in a downward spiral of ever-increasing taxation, redistribution, and desperation.

The call to redistribute everything and force every new generation to start —and to never stray too far from— zero is not new: we heard it from Morelly in 1755 and from Marx in 1848. Keynes gave these ideas the means for their gradual implementation. W. V. Harcourt and Lord Beveridge —the men who gave us the death tax and the welfare state, respectively— unwittingly gave us the tools to ensure that that every new generation is forced to start low and never strays from the starting point, the ruling political, financial, and bureaucratic elites exempted.

Yet most people who fill their minds, hearts, and mouths with "redistribution" and "equality" are convinced that it's about all humans sharing portions of the race's achievement in equal measure. Such belief is unfounded. A shrinking pie is always shared unequally and often violently.

Equality has become the new religion of the Western world, and it shares many characteristics with Western religions of the past:

- It is preached by those who do not practice it.
- It cannot be questioned, neither in its doctrine nor in its liturgy.
- All economic and intellectual resources have to be devoted to it.
- Anyone who questions either its doctrine or its liturgy is anathema (or worse, conservative).

Engels knew the true nature of his ideas: "the negation of the negation": a return to Bronze Age social arrangements based on status against the modern social arrangements based on free cooperation. And he looked forward to it. And just as he envisaged, we've been progressing backward.

Unless we stop or at least slow this regression, the end of the twenty-first century will find us socially, culturally, and financially behind our eighteenth-century forefathers. We may have only a few more gadgets to fiddle with while Rome crumbles to dust once again.

The reasons we are progressing backward are many and we find them in Marx's Decalogue at the end of the *Communist Manifesto*:

1. Agricultural policies that have turned farmers—that ancient bastion of common sense—into form-filling bureaucrats

2. Heavy progressive or graduated taxes, which have sapped the enterprising energy of anyone but the super-rich (who are, by definition exempt from taxation)

3. Death duties that remove the opportunity for intergenerational social mobility

4. Covert protectionism, which obstructs the efficient allocation of resources

5. Central banking making billionaires of those with direct access to the printing presses and beggars out of everybody else

6. Tightly controlled media that ensure the complete trashing of those who do not buy into or promote the so-called consensus

7. Misguided subsidies and privileges granted to dying or nonviable industries for political gain, draining dynamic areas (and the real jobs) of the economy

8. All-embracing welfare provisions that sap the energy of entire families, communities, regions, and even countries, often for generations

9. Dismal urban planning, which has created sinkholes of deprivation and crime

10. Education by ZIP code (or by mortgage), regardless of ability, condemning the talented rich to mediocrity and the talented poor to waste their lives, while depriving society of the abilities it both requires and possesses

At the core of this social retrogression lies the totalitarian nature of liberalism:

"People should be forced to be free"
"We want people to be free to do what we want them to do."

Don't these two statements by Rousseau and Hayek, respectively, sum up three hundred years of confusion? This totalitarian ideal is part and parcel of an idealistic or a priori system of thought, which says, "These are my ideas. I do not want to discuss them or to debate them or see them challenged. I want them implemented. In the unlikely event that I turn out to be wrong, I will come up with new ones that will be implemented without discussion, debate or challenge.

The way forward (which of course means backward) was neatly laid down by Marx in his decalogue of communism, which can be found near the end of the *Communist Manifesto*, a sneaky little pamphlet that—by its sheer succinctness, religious tone, messianic appeal, and, perhaps, a taste of the forbidden fruit— has slipped into the subconscious of the political class and forms the only source of knowledge in the field of economics and taxation in the minds of millions more, who have no knowledge of the matter.

For someone looking at our world from outer space, it may be mildly amusing that a civilization built on the Decalogue was to be destroyed by another decalogue conceived by one *a little lower than the angels*.

These transformational tools, implemented by stealth, have become rather trivial, though no less destructive:

1. The elimination or neutralization of the land-owning class, followed by complete control of the life and work of small landowners through "agricultural policies"
2. The lifelong enslavement of the middle classes through "heavy, progressive income taxes"
3. The virtual elimination of the right of inheritance for anyone except billionaires, politicians, and civil servants
4. The effective substitution of the civil servant for the spontaneous influence and collaboration of citizens in community affairs: the phenomenon of the tax exile
5. Central banking with the corruption and moral decay it brings in its wake
6. Effective control of all media through various means
7. Sweeping control of the productive economy by regulators and environmental agencies

8. Welfare provision that ensures that those who work have to work till they drop while those who don't work enjoy ever-improving standards of living on the dole (for the time being)
9. The substitution of proportional representation in place of proper systems of political accountability
10. The nationalized education system designed to provide a socializing experience instead of an educational one

The only progress ahead of us is more progress toward stagnation and decay.

CONSERVATION OR RESTORATION?

Milton Friedman said back in the 1950s,

> I never characterized myself as a conservative economist. As I understand the English language "conservative" means conserving, keeping things as they are. I don't want to keep things as they are. The true conservatives today are the people who are in favor of ever bigger government. The people who call themselves "liberal" today, the "new dealers" they are the true conservatives because they want to keep going on the same path we are going on. I would like to dismantle that. I call myself a "liberal" in the true sense of the word.

I am not a liberal, neither in the true nor in the modern sense of the word. I am a conservative and I, too, want to dismantle the monstrous and encroaching bureaucracy that rules our lives, drains all our financial and intellectual resources, and crushes any reasonable hope of improvement or even continuance of our way of life.

Nineteenth-century liberalism, feeding the body and starving the soul, and twentieth century socialism, starving the body and the soul, have despoiled our inheritance.

Why would anyone care? Russell Kirk gives us the answer, "In a world that has lost any hope of supra-natural sanction for morality, the conservative must appeal to three other passionate human interests which—among ordinary men and women—have provided the incentive to performance of duty, and reason for believing that *life is worth living*:

- the perpetuation of their own spiritual existence through the life and welfare of their children,

- the honest gratification of acquisitive appetite through accumulation and bequest of property, and
- the comforting assurance that continuity is more probable than change.

In other words, people are confidence that they participate in a natural and moral order in which they count for *more than the flies of a summer.*"

Before we start rolling back the state, we need to define what the state is to *us.*

To the true liberal, the individual is everything and the state is nothing. To the socialist, the individual is nothing and the state is everything.

To the conservative Samuel Coleridge taught us, two negative ends of the state exist:

1. its own safety, and
2. the protection of person and property.

Three positive ends stand beside these:

3. to make the means of subsistence more easy to each individual,
4. to secure for each of its members the hope of bettering his condition or that of his children, and
5. the development of faculties that are essential to his humanity—that is, to the rational and moral being.

From the first point, conservatives derive our commitment to strong defense, internal security, and forceful diplomacy.

From the second, we derive our commitment to law and order, property rights, and the enforcement of contracts.

From the third, we derive our commitment to free trade, to free enterprise, and to home ownership. (Socialism, corporatism, and protectionism not only make people *less free*, they also make them *poorer* and desperate.)

From the fourth, we derive our support for families, for free (in every sense of the word) education, the encouragement and protection of individual savings and the rejection in principle of inheritance taxes and other limitations to the bequest of property. And from the fifth point, we derive our commitment to freedom of learning, to freedom of speech, to religious freedom, to political freedom, to freedom of association, and of course to economic freedom, *upon which all our other freedoms depend.*

It doesn't take a genius to realize that conservatism has points in common with both true liberalism and modern-day liberalism, but the rationale, the motivations, the intentions, and most importantly the *outcomes* are always different.

We want to conserve our country, our culture, our liberty, our prosperity, and our laws—in sum, our humanity—because *this is our inheritance,* what we *are.* But, far more importantly, because *they are good for us.* It is never to ensure the realization of an *ideal.*

We do not have an ideology. A fanciful "new order" concocted in the mind of a thinker with no practical reference to the reality on the ground will destroy our liberty and our prosperity and will trample our laws underfoot. This is a mathematical certainty, besides being exemplified over the past few thousand years.

This is not chauvinism. Nor is it particular to Western countries; conservatism is as valid an intellectual position in Washington as it is in Moscow or Beijing, in Canterbury or Mecca, in Tel Aviv or Tehran.

Conservatism is a moral and intellectual proposition "that is tried by experience and sprung from our condition."

Liberty, prosperity, and the rule of law—our inheritance—are always at risk, sometimes more imminently and sometimes less. The history of the great English-speaking nations over the past two hundred years is one of remarkable progress and even more remarkable *conservation.*

Critics of conservatism have claimed over the years that conservatives are impelled to action only against imminent threat to their values. This is not so: the mere survival of political parties that claim to uphold the conservative impulse even in the face of unrelenting onslaught is an extraordinary achievement. Extraordinary, but insufficient.

We could have easily continued the social and economic downward spiral that characterized life in Britain and America in the 1932–1982 period, but we did not. We could have learned to live with the Soviet Union as we do now with North Korea, but we did not.

While the Left spoke extensively about the *orderly management of decline,* conservatives got to work and stopped the rot.

Critics also claim that the 1980s conservative revival was just a blip in a process of social disintegration that cannot be stopped, let alone reversed.

Maybe. But people –back then– saw with their very eyes the fruits of collectivism, and they knew something was wrong:

- The audacity of the labor movement and its associates
- The arrogance of the economists and government officials
- The depressing smugness of the political consensus
- The trampling of Western interests underfoot by every Third World dictator
- The deficits, the inflation, the unemployment, and the loss of hope
- The orderly management of decline, which was presented as both inevitable and desirable

Sadly, no sooner had we gotten out of the mess, we went back to our bad old tricks. Government spending and indebtedness went through the roof, the number of civil servants and welfare recipients escalated, currency manipulation became once again the order of the day, and now we find ourselves again facing:

- The audacity of the labor movement and its associates (now almost exclusively concentrated on the public sector, having previously bankrupted most of our heavy industry)
- The arrogance of the economists and government officials
- The depressing smugness of the political consensus
- The trampling of Western interests underfoot by every Third World dictator
- The deficits, the inflation, the unemployment, and the loss of hope
- The orderly management of decline, which is again presented as both inevitable and desirable

The *party of progress* has long run out of ideas. Whether we find ourselves in 1932 or in 1972 or in 1982 depends on what the *party of order* does next.

WHERE DO WE START?

It would be mildly poetic on my part to propose a new decalogue of true progress to replace the Marxist decalogue of retrogression and decay.

1. The abolition of all taxes, controls, and intervention in the area of agriculture.
2. A low, flat, or mildly progressive income, corporation, and capital gains tax.
3. The elimination of inheritance taxes and all restrictions to and regulations of entail.
4. Equal tax treatment for all. (elimination of withholding taxes)
5. Truly independent central banking.
6. Careful privatization of all state-owned media outlets.
7. Elimination of all state intervention in the area of industrial policy except during a national emergency.
8. Intelligent privatization of Social Security provisions.
9. Limitation of population targeting to protected historical or natural areas.
10. The transformation of all state-owned or state-run educational establishments into foundation or charter institutions, run by the community or private enterprise

Over the next few years, we need to concentrate on the areas of taxation, Social Security provision, education, and central banking.

What follows is an outline of what I believe should be done to ensure that liberty, prosperity, and the rule of law live to fight another day.

Taxation

"No taxation by Royal prerogative."
English Bill of Rights, 1689

"No taxation without representation."
American revolutionary slogan, 1750s

"A heavy progressive or graduated income tax."
Communist Manifesto, 1848

Who do you think has won the argument?

The issue of taxation is guaranteed to get people hyperventilating. It is commonly said that true liberals see taxation as voluntary contributions to defray the cost of the state while modern liberals see it as a means to redress social inequality: to make "the rich" pay their fair share. Both statements are absurd: taxation was never voluntary, while converting investment funds – *taxing the rich*– into ordinary expenditure is guaranteed to prevent wealth and job creation, thus increasing and not decreasing the chasm between the haves and the have-nots.

At the root of the issue is our misunderstanding of what government and the state are and what they are there to do. This is not a trivial matter.

- *Government* is political *direction and control* exercised *over* the members, citizens, or inhabitants of communities, societies, and states; it directs the affairs of a state or community.
- The *state* is a nation itself, considered as a political entity and organized for civil rule and government.
- A *tax* is a contribution for the support of *a government* required of persons, groups, or businesses within the domain of that government.

Now, governments came into existence almost everywhere as the result of a military or tribal chief organizing an army and taking over a territory for the *fiscal exploitation* of its people and resources. As time progresses and rulers are "tamed," either out of expediency or by armed rebellion, mechanisms are put in place to protect the life, liberty, and property of the inhabitants (with wildly different degrees of success). Over time, such arrangements or institutions become what we call "the state."

On the other hand, taxes predate the state by a long margin and are most likely the reason governments were instituted to begin with: as a protection racket. Taxes are a prerogative of government, and this prerogative is born out the overwhelming force the government has at its disposal.

The state is there to *do the collection* of taxes and, on rare occasions, to *mitigate the harshness* of their application. In the case of England, a large number of rebellions and compromises between king and country determined by 1689 that the sovereign could not exact tribute without the consent of the *representatives of the people who would bear the burden of taxation*. This did not deny the power of the government to demand what it wanted from the taxpayer; it only made it clear that the taxpayer would reserve the right to reach a compromise between what the government wanted (which often exceeds the country's ability to pay) and what the country is willing and capable of paying.

The English in America—that is, the Americans—knew this all too well, and they rebelled against unprecedented royal exactions in 1776, just as their forefathers had done back home in 1642.

It was not the lack of representation (which could have been easily resolved), but the lack of *precedent* that prompted them to action, making the American War of Independence a conservative revolution.

The eighteenth-century philosophers and, through them, the modern mass-educated, understood none of this: they decided that the constitution of England separated the powers of the state in three—executive, legislative, and judiciary—and that everyone else should do the same and live happily ever after. A Genevan absentee father, by the name of Rousseau even had the audacity of announcing that the sovereign in fact had a "contract" with the people to protect them and their lives, their liberties, and their property in exchange of voluntary contributions. Nonsense! The only impulse to protect on the part of the people in charge came from the obvious fact that if they do not protect their possessions, somebody else would have done it for them.

For thousands of years, sovereigns have taxed the life out of their vassals to achieve their aims. The people never had a say in any of this, being largely indifferent as to who was in charge. They would be fiscally exploited by them anyway.

The power of taxation on the part of whatever individual or group of individuals happen to be in charge comes from their ability to inflict pain—the power to direct all the resources of the country against the individuals who refuse to pay—not from any pretended contract. But the confusion of the philosophers did not end there. The eighteenth-century philosophers decided that, since the government (in the form of a sovereign king) was not fulfilling his contract, the people should become the sovereign.

Marx went a step further, endorsing that the proletariat –that is the blue collar element of the working class− be raised to the position of the ruling class. How wrong can somebody actually be without being declared insane? In all fairness, it took the Western political class about a century to realize what had actually happened: Instead of having an incompetent and megalomaniac king wasting everybody's money on pet projects and a lavish court (and everybody's time with minute regulation), they got an incompetent and megalomaniac political and bureaucratic class wasting everybody's money on pet projects and a lavish court (and everybody's time with minute regulation).

Whether by divine right or by majority rule, taxation is *always* without the consent of the taxpayer.

The government can be our servant *if it chooses to be*, but it can also choose to be our master. (It is always the choice of the guy in charge, not the *people*.) The state has become so vast and unwieldy that the cost of government has become a threat to liberty, prosperity, and the rule of law.

We had	*We have*
The Crown	A professional politician
The House of Lords	Professional politicians
The House of Commons	Professional politicians
The Supreme Court	Professional politicians
The Gold Standard	Professional politicians

"WHO WATCHES THE WATCHMEN?"

The person in charge—provided he gets along with his fellow politicians in government, in the highest court, and in the central bank—has *de facto* the power to

- spend as much as he wants on whatever he wants,
- tax as much as he wants,
- borrow as much as he wants,
- print as much money as he wants,
- cajole individuals to give money to his supporters and projects,
- coerce the population into buying specific products and services,
- decide what can be bought or sold and at what price, and
- persecute, destroy the reputation of, bankrupt, or jail anyone who does not agree with him.

How did we get here? How did these philosophers manage to convince the world of such nonsense? The answer is simple: flattery.

They told us that all virtues—namely, chastity, temperance, charity, diligence, patience, kindness, and humility (you know, all the characteristics we *rarely* display)—are part of our nature or the result of reason and education. Therefore, they could be spread and extended indefinitely by more reason and education. They also told us that lust, gluttony, greed, sloth, wrath, envy, and pride (you know, all the traits we *all too often* display) are the unnatural creation of depraved institutions. If they could be said to exist, they could be eradicated through reason and education.

There is no controlling our leaders; we need leaders who can (and want to) control themselves.

Leaders who believe the people should have the state as servant and not as master.

We need good leaders, but where can we find them? If they don't exist, they will have to be created.

As the English found out in 1642, there is only one way to restrain a wayward sovereign: by controlling the purse strings. Reason never has and never will do the trick. Our present, slightly deranged generation of politicians cannot and will not control themselves. They hate the countries they were elected to rule, they hate their people's liberties, they hate their people's prosperity, they hate their countries' laws, they hate and hate and hate and hate.

But this generation of leaders will pass away. Will the next one be better or worse? It's up to us. I hope for a new generation of leaders that loves our country, our people, our customs, our laws, our liberties, our industry, our values, our inheritance, and that are proud of the inheritance we have given to the world. But when this generation of lovers of liberty, prosperity, and the rule of law comes to power, what should they do with our taxes?

That is a good question that begs another: do we still believe that "the government of the people by the people and for the people are shall not perish from the earth"? We do? Then we first need to define exactly what we mean by "the people," since we are to govern for them and be governed by them.

We the people

In some languages, the word *people* has a distinct meaning. The words *peuple*, *pueblo*, and *popolo* conjure in French, Hispanic, and Italian minds a very distinct image: the common folk. Remove anybody who is anybody for whatever reason and what is left is *el pueblo*. It follows that in those cultures the government "of the people" may well be "for the people" but never "by the people," since the mere act of governing sets one apart from *le peuple*.

British and American enthusiasts of all things continental found themselves at a loss when dealing with European ideas: a distinct idea of "the people" as separate from, er, the people was yet to be formed in their countries. Statisticians and economists provided the answer: calculate the average income. Those below (that is, the bottom 50 percent) are "the people"; those above are not. The transformation of the state into some sort of bureaucratic Robin Hood was underway.

Legend has it that the Roman Emperor Caligula once led his army into battle with a Germanic tribe. Since the tribe didn't turn up for a fight, the emperor ordered half his troops to pretend to be tribesmen and fight against the Roman army and lose. He then returned to Rome as a victor to the horror and dismay of his citizens, who realized he had killed half of his own army.

Our modern-day Caligulas have divided the country in two by the diabolical power of Excel. And now the political and bureaucratic elites sit high above the battlefield, stealing from the rich 50 percent and giving to the poor 50 percent while lavishing the bulk of the booty on their own ranks.

You see, the richest half couldn't possibly be trusted to *give* the money to the bottom 50 percent. Nor indeed could the bottom 50 percent be trusted with the money if it were given to them in the form of cash: they would spend it on what they want, not on what they *should* want. The monies are distributed in the form of things the economists and other bureaucrats believe the bottom 50 percent *should* desire. This is achieved by employing another several million bureaucrats and granting lavish government contracts to compliant enterprises.

The Romans realized Caligula was mad and sent him packing. Can we do the same with our economists? We can only live in hope.

From the most successful entrepreneur to the street sweeper, from the most famous media star to the technician, we are all "the people." And we do not need a vast and expensive bureaucracy that saps the life of the nation to create the illusion that the great among us are the enemy and that the rest of us have a duty to hate them.

If and when we decide to send the diabolical Excel-men packing, the taxation system should return to its *legitimate* function: defraying the necessary expenses of the state.

Economic leveling may be necessary from time to time, but it is not and should never be allowed to become the sole or even the main purpose of government action.

We have a vast array of taxes and technology at our disposal, but the guiding principle should be this: do not discourage what is good for us, do not encourage what is bad for us.

The more you tax something, the less of it you get. (Especially true in the case of jobs, Ricardo notwithstanding)

"Good" to the conservative is anything that furthers the case of liberty, prosperity, and the rule of law. "Bad" is anything that detracts from them—namely,

- if growing-businesses are a good thing,
- if new businesses are a good thing,
- if new products and services are a good thing,
- if new jobs and employment opportunities are a good thing,
- the capital formation (and the financier and the entrepreneur) that makes them possible is a good thing.

Spending is good; saving is great.

If an efficient, effective, streamlined and low-cost government is good, cheap government and a balanced budget is our only security against tyranny in the long run.

What the political class doesn't waste, the people can spend or invest.

If a sound currency and banking system is good, the government should never be tempted to destroy it by overstretching its finances.

The surest way to destroy a nation is to debauch its currency.

Once we realize that the taxation system should not be used to discourage what most of us *agree is good for us,* taxation doesn't hold many secrets. But we need to remember the words of Milton Friedman to that effect: **"The burden of**

taxation is the sum of all government spending, regardless of how it appears to be financed."In practical terms, this means that whatever the government spends is exactly what people will be prevented from spending or investing.

A good taxation system will vary from time to time and from place to place, but it will almost invariably include a small number of taxes, which

- together are sufficient to defray government expenditure through the economic cycle;
- individually and in combination are cheap and easy to administer and to pay;
- cause minimum disruption in the decision-making and wealth-creation processes;
- are perceived to be fair by both taxpayers and the public;
- do not unduly channel such a large proportion of the national income that it imperils wealth and job creation.

Whatever combination is chosen, it is likely to include

- a sales tax,
- a personal income tax,
- a corporation or corporate income tax,
- a capital gains tax,
- a municipal or council tax, and
- Social Security contributions.

A SALES TAX, NOT A VALUE ADDED TAX.

A sales tax ranges from 3 to 6 percent is charged on goods and on utilities. This is easy and cheap to collect by retailers and electrical utilities, telecom operators, gas suppliers, and so on. A rate in the range above would minimize the desire for evasion and not unduly impede economic activity. A tax on services that are usually performed in person, such as plumbing and cleaning, is likely to be evaded, thus creating a corrupt, gray economy we could best do without.

The so-called value added tax, which taxes every stage of the production and commercialization cycle, is astronomically expensive to administer and tends to distort the entire value chain. It is a very powerful disincentive to consumption (and therefore production), thus negatively affecting investment, employment, and overall economic activity. It also is a powerful disincentive to investment and is so burdensome that *the incentive to evade it corrupts societies from top to bottom* creating vast untaxed economies.

Value added taxes destroy economic activity for sums much larger than they would ever collect. They are an across-the-board hindrance to prosperity and an inexhaustible source of corruption and waste. Politically, however, value added taxes are very difficult to remove once implemented. Those on the left love them, because they believe they fall only on the salaried middle class. Those on the right love them, because they believe they fall only on the salaried middle class. The salaried middle class loves them because they think they fall on everyone else.

If it's already been implemented, it should be removed. If not, it should never be started.

A PERSONAL INCOME TAX

A flat or mildly progressive personal income tax should range from, say, 0 percent for the lower 20 percent of earners, 20 percent for the following 60 percent of earners, 30 percent for the top 20 percent of earners—or preferably: 0 percent, 10 percent, and 20 percent respectively.

The top rate should never be allowed to creep above 30 percent.

A large number of individuals would be horrified at these rates, thinking them too low. There should be provisions in tax returns to allow individuals to pay as much as they want over and above the official rate. Those who feel guilty about their financial well-being could increase their contribution to the state as much as they'd like.

Politically, this will take some convincing. With social mobility at the lowest in three hundred years and heading lower, the chances are that if you are on a good salary, so were your parents and grandparents. It was just as natural for you to go to college as it was for the third-generation welfare recipient to depend on welfare.

While high and even very high personal income taxes are unlikely to deter the "lucky ones" from following in the family tradition of financial success (even if it means emigrating), it has an enormous impact on the millions who should be striving to better their condition but realize that there is little if any point in trying.

Our current tax structure is not the cause of social immobility (which is largely the result of ill-conceived welfare arrangements and even worse education provision), but it has certainly removed the main financial incentive for social advancement: the chance of a better life. The sooner we get our income taxes back to where they should be, the sooner we will get the economy —and society—moving again.

A CORPORATION TAX

A corporation tax never surpassing that of our most competitive comparable economies, currently about 22 percent. Corporation taxes are a legal fiction: corporations (a legal fiction themselves) by definition cannot suffer a tax; only people can (in the form of reduced income, quality of life, employment opportunities, and higher prices, usually all at the same time).

Corporation income tax exists for various reasons: the general economic illiteracy that leads people to believe that corporations are rich, the sheer ease for the taxing authority, and the tax-exempt nature of so many shareholders. Taxing both the corporation's profits and the dividends paid to individuals is a juvenile display of misinformed class warfare, unworthy of a democracy.

Politically, the case should be made in no uncertain terms; if we really want more jobs and more money for welfare programs, pushing employers (and tax revenue) out of the country is a really bad strategy.

This will not convince a committed anti-capitalist, since his objective is to starve the population into submission. But most politicians are more interested in their careers than in fighting the class wars of eighteenth-century France or nineteenth-century Germany.

A CAPITAL GAINS TAX ON INDIVIDUALS

Capital gains taxes are so easy to evade they should probably be taken out of the statute book as a practical matter. Removing capital gains tax altogether would be contentious: people believe this tax *punishes* the rich. In reality it is a clever devise to keep the super-rich that way —they would never find themselves in need of selling their assets and becoming liable to the tax— while those who are not super-rich hand over to the government what little money they have managed to accumulate.

Capital gains taxes levied on corporations are simply a source of economic inefficiency; they serve no useful purpose and should be eliminated. Only the misguided belief popularized by Ricardo and Marx that capital accumulation is *bad* for the workers (since more and more jobs mean lower and lower wages in their topsy-turvy version of events) justifies this economically suicidal form of taxation.

We'll have to do a lot of teaching before we can get rid of this hindrance to prosperity.

A MUNICIPAL TAX

This is a very complex issue. Conservatives believe that taxing and spending should take place as close to the citizen as possible: there is only one way for the citizens to ensure they are getting their money's worth and that is to keep taxes and spending at the lowest possible level of government. Others see municipal taxation as either a proxy "wealth tax" or an extension of the personal income tax.

The taxation of individual households in a community should be for the local residents to decide.

But there is a catch: the municipality can never be allowed to grow to the point in which the citizen loses track of what is going on. If the municipality is allowed to become too large —usually in the quest for economies of scale— it stops serving its purpose of preserving practical democracy and grassroots accountability. For example, if a voluntary councilor suddenly appeared down the road with a new chauffer driven Rolls Royce, his neighbor would notice. If an unknown official from a distant government department did just that, no one would care or have a clue as who he is or how he came about his money.

As for the municipal taxation of businesses, national or state upper limits may be necessary from time to time to avoid abuses on the part of a voracious local authority, whose deleterious effects may only be felt when the damage to the local economy has become irreversible.

Miscellaneous

Taxes on energy, on financial transactions, on insurance products are easy to collect but heavily distortive of economic activity. The ease with which they may be collected blinds the government to the damage they do to the economy.

Also, they are very popular with environmentalists because these taxes hinder economic activity, with the left, because they seem to be manna from heaven; and with politicians in general, because these taxes do not fall onto any particular constituency who could complain about them.

Conclusion on general taxation

The burden of taxation and of government expenditure has increased dramatically in the past 150 years. This is due to three separate phenomena.

First, there doesn't seem to be a single area of human endeavor that is not ripe for regulation and control. This control requires vast and ever-expanding bureaucracies whose sheer cost and interference reduce economic activity and in turn require heavier taxation and indebtedness to be maintained.

Second, the removal of all property and tax status qualifications on the right to vote which, while having very positive social effects, has produced a very strange situation: those who actually have to defray the cost of the state are a small minority that is hardly, if ever, represented in government.

Those who suffer taxation indirectly in the form of higher prices, lower economic activity, fewer jobs, and a reduced quality of life have no means of associating the size and the cost of the state with their predicament. The truly bizarre spectacle of unemployed youth in Europe demanding *less* capitalism (as if it were possible) and *higher* taxes—which, by definition, will have to come from not carrying out the investments and the spending that could have led to their being employed—is a testament to this astonishing confusion.

Finally, the modern obsession with redistribution of income which leads to less investment and fewer jobs and therefore the need for higher taxes and more redistribution, in a never ending cycle of stagnation and decay, and is a devise to ensure that not a single penny should ever escape from the hands of government. This is slowly but surely making Marx's sweeping away of the *old* conditions of existence a very tangible and disheartening reality for the young.

People crave the old conditions of existence Marx wanted to sweep away: a job or a shop, a liberal profession, a house, a family, a car, a pet, a few holidays, and hope for their future and that of our children.

We are throwing away these *capitalist* conditions of existence in the name of economic equality. And something tells me that the manna from heaven will be slow to arrive.

Income is only *distributed* in a statistical chart. In the real world, income has to be earned.

SOCIAL SECURITY PROVISION

"Social Security," born partly out of misguided humanitarianism and partly out of political opportunism is nothing more than a "regressive tax on wages and on job creation"; "sold to the public as an insurance scheme" "by imaginative packaging and deceptive labeling."
"It is a combination of a bad tax system with a bad way of distributing welfare"

Milton Friedman

Philosophically, Social Security *contributions* and the myriads of *benefits* that flow out of it without rhyme or reason are the economic manifestation of Ricardo's belief that a tax on wages, increases wages, and Marx's dictum "from each according to their ability, to each according to their need." (Marx lifted the latter from the book of Exodus, where God distributes food among the Israelites, allowing each to collect according to their *abilities* but ensuring by divine intervention that everyone received according to their *appetite*.)

In the biblical story, God was distributing his own stuff, not someone else's *and*, just as importantly, He limited the miracle to basic foodstuff (which He did not attempt to ration) in the middle of a national emergency (the forty years of wondering in the desert). Social Security is a permanent devise of redistribution for its own sake. It is not a safety net, or anything vaguely resembling one. Social security is far more ambitious than God ever was: it aims to provide for everybody's needs by taking from everybody *else*.

MARCELO PESCI

Conservatives do not hate the safety net, as certain overexcited Hollywood stars would have you believe. They realized decades ago that Social Security is not social and it doesn't provide security. And it is anything *but* a safety net.

As it stands today, Social Security —in Britain and America— it collects 11 percent of the salary from the employee and 11 percent of the salary from the employer. To the financially literate, this means a 20 percent flat income tax on salaries levied on top of income tax.

Now, if this is a tax, why the need to show us we are buying several insurance products with it? Originally it was not meant to be a tax, but the *enforced purchase of a series of insurance and savings products*. Fears that too many individuals would fail to provide for themselves —in unemployment, ill health or old age— motivated the government to create a national monopoly—and the accompanying national compulsion—to that effect.

Forcing people to buy insurance from a commercial provider would not have gone through a constitutional court a hundred years ago (as it does now), plus this was the era of national monopolies, which were expected to bring enormous efficiency and savings by eliminating *wasteful* competition.

Here are the benefits we are allegedly buying with 20 percent of our salaries:

- life insurance, of sorts,
- death in service insurance,
- unemployment insurance,
- disability insurance,
- retirement benefits,
- medical insurance,
- critical illness insurance,
- and so on.

For the vast majority of the population, such programs could be easily managed either in a commercial, for-profit environment or by a suitable organization with the relevant technical expertise, charging a fixed amount for the service and with contracts awarded on a competitive basis and reviewed every few years.

This would free the government bureaucracy to take care of those individuals who—by virtue of physical incapacity, intellectual limitations, or lifestyle choices such as drug addiction—are or have made themselves permanently or temporarily unemployable or uninsurable. No one should be left behind, but "whatever each man can separately do, without trespassing upon others, he has a right to do for himself."

Competition, far from being wasteful; is the most effective incentive to innovation quality improvements, price reduction, cost reduction, and the improvement of working conditions. Private initiative should free trillions of dollars of investment potential in the economy, which should provide new incentives to work, to invest, and to save, improving lives and opening a new world of possibilities. The market operation and minimum coverage, as well as the capital adequacy of the providers, should be regulated. After that people should be free to choose.

For example, workers should be able to build an unemployment fund from a government-mandated minimum of, say, six months to a maximum of eighteen months. Once the fund has been built up, the worker would get to keep the portion of his income that otherwise would have gone to cover his unemployment insurance. The fund could be invested, with the profits increasing the worker's safety net. Moreover, people would be free to use the fund for career breaks or retraining and either to take it out as a lump sum or to add it to a pension fund upon retirement. The same goes for all the other forms of insurance and savings products over which the government holds a monopoly.

This would allow freedom, encourage financial literacy, raise self-awareness, and promote responsibility, and also focus the state and the charitable sector on *helping those who actually need helping* instead of wasting billions "helping" everybody else while allowing the vulnerable to fall through the cracks—or be condemned to a life of idleness and despair. The use of compulsion is an acknowledgement that a small but significant minority may be unable or unwilling to make necessary arrangements and that the taxpayer will have to fork out the cash. This is an argument for compulsion, not for national monopolies.

What's more, if it is decided that people should purchase the various kinds of insurance and savings products described above, there is no reason to demand that they should cost a specific percentage of someone's salary. Fair competition in the provision of these services would enable people to choose the best deals available for the level of protection they want and enable the industry to provide affordable products.

Marx is dead. Get over it.

I have serious reservations regarding the use of compulsion across the board. A twenty-one year old would be much better off using his income to save for a deposit on a house than putting money aside for when he reaches eighty-seven. But, by and large, having identified the need for compulsion, there is no benefit to be extracted from making the system a government monopoly.

SOCIETY AS A MACHINE: WHAT'S IT ALL ABOUT?

For millennia, religious and charitable institutions have aimed to provide relief for those in severe distress through no fault of their own: abandoned babies, orphans, the severely handicapped, the sick, the elderly poor, and other unfortunate individuals. The mechanization of industry starting in the 1750s was bound to foster the emergence of social and economic schools that would seek to apply the principles of industry to society at large, including relief.

In industry: Acquire the machine, install it, prepare it for production, use it productively, perform necessary maintenance, dispose of it at the end of its useful life, and replace it with new machinery.

In society: Receive "human resources" in a standardized fashion, vaccinate them, prepare them for production in standardized schools, use them productively, and finally warehouse them (at the expense of their peers) after those productive years have elapsed. Dispose of them efficiently and humanely by means of a cost-effective mass health-care system.

Maternity clinics, mass vaccination programs, nationalized systems of education, a carefully coordinated mixture of public sector and private sector employment opportunities (welfare provisions and prisons, for those unable, unwilling, or too violent to work), retirement provisions for the elderly, health and medical care provision for the elderly, and state owned and run cemeteries and crematoria are the universal manifestation of this approach.

From the factory to the scrapheap.
From the cradle to the grave.

Many of these services existed before industrialization, but it never crossed our ancestors' minds to have the government run them. Yet one may wonder if there is anything wrong with such arrangements?

There is one serious objection from the conservative point of view—not to the existence of such arrangements but to the means for their provision. The underlying assumption behind all these national enterprises was simple: the belief that an omniscient, omnipresent, and omnipotent government department, whose legitimacy, authority and good intentions could never be questioned or challenged, was the most qualified to redress the giant evils of squalor, ignorance, want, idleness, and disease in a free society.

In a free society, freeing people from the need to think or worry about basic needs would in turn free them to concentrate on what really matters—presumably the higher intellectual, spiritual, political, and artistic aspects of the human experience.

What no one took into account was that "small" freedoms, such as choosing schools, doctors, pension arrangements, utility providers, supermarkets, brands, and prices, constitutes all or almost all the opportunities most people have to exercise freedom and to benefit from that exercise: we can't all be politicians.

A population free from the need to think for itself won't find any kind of freedom—much less *the economic freedom on which all of our other freedoms depend*—worth the hassle.

Come on, surely losing a bit of freedom to get all these advantages is worth the pain? Yes—but no, I'm afraid.

The same people whose freedoms have been eloped in the name of efficiency or rather, simplicity are expected to continue to maintain the *system of liberty* that makes all those advantages *economically viable* and that places politicians and civil servants under the *constructive obligation* to provide them. In other words, the low taxes; unfettered industry, commerce, and finance; the protection of property; and the enforcement of contracts—that is, the economic freedom upon which all of our freedoms depend—will have to be defended every four years at the ballot box by people who have never had the opportunity to exercise *any freedom* and who have no way of knowing that on these very freedoms their prosperity depends (as do all the government programs paid for by that prosperity).

Freeing people from the need to think and to provide for themselves is the opposite of freeing them; it would be more appropriately described as "easing them into dependency." And it is absurd to expect them to show anything but contempt for the liberties—and the people—that make their prosperity possible. Over time their political masters will treat them with the same contempt they have shown for their enterprising fellows.

Keep this in mind as we analyze the next topic: medical care.

MEDICAL CARE

This is a very hot and emotionally charged topic. And it should be. Our lives and those of our loved ones often depend on it.

At least in the United States, it is also the last piece of the jigsaw I call "machine society"—how a scientifically planned polity decides what machines should be repaired and to what extent, and what machines should not. Conservatives reject the liberal idea of the machine-society about as much as they detest the communist human-farm. But this *logicalism* in society is here to stay, simply because too many well-paid government jobs and too many lucrative government contracts depend on it. So we should limit the damage these vast compulsions inflict on our liberty, our prosperity, and the rule of law.

It doesn't take a genius to notice that the greatest amount of medical care the average individual will ever need will be on his run-up to the grave as doctors are trying to save his life. It takes even less insight to realize that this is most likely to happen in old age, precisely when the machine-society has the least number of future uses for him.

It follows that insurance is probably not the most suitable vehicle for the provision of medical care and all other related care in old age. Unsurprisingly, those who want the state to be everything and to do everything want a national enterprise to achieve this; not to look after those in need but to look after everyone.

Even a cursory look at history shows that nationalized industries are the worst possible way to achieve this—or any objective other than war. Any half-decent book on basic economics would list the problems with monopoly, such as inefficiency, inequity, and political abuse.

But some far more important objections are observable only to the trained eye and are not economic: the behavior of suppliers, managers, and the workforce.

- Suppliers will not only use their influence to get the best deal at taxpayer's expense; they will seek to have friendly executives appointed to run and to supervise the national monopoly, ensuring the public a permanent raw deal and plum contracts for themselves.
- Managers are political appointees whose interests would never be and could never be in line with those of the entity they run or the clients the entity serves. They have no incentive or authority to challenge suppliers and even less incentive or authority to challenge unions and other stakeholders.

- The workforce is quickly unionized, gaining the combined power of being the monopoly supplier of labor to the monopolist supplier of services. This means having a stranglehold on both the management and the government at large.

Any attempt at political control will spectacularly backfire: managers, suppliers and the trade unions, all have far greater power of patronage than any particular politician or political party. In no time, those politicians assigned to control the nationalized industry, will be on the payroll of those they are expected to supervise.

In health care, this combination is literally lethal, as many have found out to their cost. But there is a more subtle and infinitely more important point. What few people in the nationalized-versus-private-health-care debate are aware of is something Marx would have spotted immediately: once the decision-making process about medical services or products to buy has been transferred from each individual patient seeking her best personal interest to one politician or bureaucrat seeking her own political interest, almost all advances in medicine stop dead in their tracks.

Allow me to elaborate: Let's say a laboratory is developing a new drug that can save lives. Five years into the trial, we know it can extend lives by six months in 5 percent of the cases at a cost of 100,000 dollars. If I could be helped by such a devise and I happen to have the money or the medical insurance to cover the cost, I will probably decide to give it a try.

Over the years, the product may be dramatically improved and/or its cost reduced. But maybe not.

Knowing that people would be free to purchase their product, which in turn would require extensive advertising to raise public awareness, the lab may engage in its development, which may or may not lead to further advances but which will certainly cost vast sums of money, whether successful or not.

If the decision making is done by a *rational* government official, the answer would most likely be either no or a request for several years of statistically demonstrable cost-effectiveness. Of course this could never be provided because no one would be allowed to use the product in the first place.

Such regulatory agency would never risk a public-opinion backlash by allowing labs to advertise a product they have no intention or resources to purchase. Allowing individuals with the resources to buy the product at their own expense would establish a politically explosive disparity in life expectancy after treatment between the haves and the have-nots.

So the advertising would be banned and the *development* will simply never take place.

This is why, if every country on Earth (or the United States) went for full nationalization of health care, apart from any accidental discovery, all advances of the medical sciences would stop dead in their tracks. And this, my dear friends, is a *mathematical certainty*.

Now, a totally different stance is to say, "Hey, there is no chance medicine or pharmacology will advance another inch. And besides, everything they do only seems to increase life expectancy and therefore health care expense." Although I do not agree with this, I can understand the argument. But remember that Morelly wanted full nationalization of everything (and with it, tacitly, the end of technological progress) in 1755, Marx in 1848, Lenin in 1917, Keynes in 1936, Mao in 1949, Castro in 1958, and Pol Pot in 1975, to name but a few.

However, the case for nationalization is not without merit.

- Following global (or American) nationalization, in a few years all medicines would go off patent and retail for little more than the cost of materials.
- Labs will be dismantled; scientists will find new endeavors, possibly making hospital staff cheaper and more abundant for a while; and universities will stop the stream of new scientists in these areas for lack of employment opportunities.
- The medical sciences have achieved a lot already.

But the dates above still loom large in my mind: we thought we had achieved more than enough in 1755.

I believe it is our collective duty to look after those fellow humans who cannot look after themselves, but a government-owned, government-run, national monopoly is not the best way to achieve this. To the conservative the words of Edmund Burke loom large:

"Whatever each man can separately do, without trespassing upon others, he has a right to do for himself."

Notice the use of the word right instead of duty. This may seem an odd choice to the modern reader, but this is just a reminder that, just a few years back, the exercise of liberty was not a chore.

So for the sake of our sanity, our well-being, our liberty, and the progress of the medical sciences, let's make national monopolies the last option.

EDUCATION

"Free education for all children in public schools, and the abolition of child labor in its present form" reads the tenth commandment of communism. Free, compulsory and uniform education for all had been an aspiration of certain segments of society even before industrialization.

By *free* we mean a government monopoly, since we are not free to refuse it nor are we free to choose what we teach or what we learn. By *free* we mean free of charge but otherwise unfree. The reasons for this compulsion are at times humanitarian, commercial, political, and practical—namely,

- Humanitarian: to provide even the poorest with basic tools for social, moral, and intellectual advancement (the "non-poor" 70 or 80 percent of the population could always educate their children by paying for it)
- Commercial: to provide industry and commerce with a constant stream of disciplined workers with similar abilities who would not demand a premium for the monies and time spent acquiring them (they did not directly spend a penny nor were they free to do anything else with their time)
- Political: our society is so advanced, prosperous, sophisticated, and complex that only citizens well versed in these complexities could be able to maintain it for any length of time
- Practical: because kids in schools free the parents to work and because long schooling keeps the younger generation from putting pressure on the labor market, enables the government to make sure only certain ideas make their way into people's minds, creates millions of jobs for teachers, administrators, consultants, and bureaucrats, and so on.

All of the above except *making sure only certain ideas make their way into people's minds* can be efficiently and effectively achieved without government monopolies.

Education is "the art or process of imparting or acquiring general knowledge, developing the powers of reasoning and judgment and generally of *preparing oneself or others intellectually for mature life*." From the very definition of education, it follows that having some idea of what an individual's "mature life" is likely to be is the first step toward designing a program that would be useful to him and society.

In a state-dominated system, government officials (elected or otherwise) decide whose children will be prepared for the top, the upper middle, the lower middle, the bottom, and the underbelly of the socioeconomic pyramid.

The education system can be the most progressive or the most regressive instrument in the reformer's arsenal.

For the hundred or so years of liberal (as in truly liberal) educational ascendancy (1870–1970), the education system was an extraordinarily progressive devise that gave all those with a combination of ability and attitude a chance to make it regardless of birth or wealth, by providing *general schooling* for everyone and *academically advanced schooling* for the intellectually gifted, whether rich or poor.

From the end of World War II to this day, there has been an unrelenting attack on any truly progressive aspect of the education system. The future life of any child born in Britain or America today depends almost exclusively on his or her address—that is, on the size of the mortgage on his or her parents' home, irrespective of personal ability or attitude.

But, important as it is, it would be a mistake to concentrate exclusively on advancing the lot of the "gifted poor," as the liberals did a century and a half ago. As Margaret Thatcher wrote,

"We are all unequal. No one, thank heavens, is quite like anyone else. But to us every human being is *equally important*."

To the conservative, the person in the top 5 percent of intellectual ability (or, indeed, income) has as much a right to maximize his potential and live his life as he chooses as the person in the bottom 5 percent or in any segment in between.

But the maximization of these individuals' potential can come only from an honest assessment of what the potential is and not from the *monstrous* fiction of intellectual and attitudinal equality, which is the underlying assumption behind our one-size-fits-all modern schools. It is monstrous because it is so cruel.

As far as I know, only the German-speaking nations have developed or maintained a system of secondary education that generally provides separate schooling for the four main groups of academic ability, with a fifth type of school for students with serious learning difficulties or other issues. In Britain and America, people have learned to live with the "monstrous fiction" of intellectual equality largely by the migration of those families with ample means toward school districts and catchment areas with the best schools in them—or, less often, by going private.

This creates various separate problems:

First, having money is no guarantee of ability or attitude, so the best schooling available is lavished on those who can pay for prime locations but who don't necessarily possess the ability or the attitude to go as far as the best could go. The best schools are held back by mediocrity, even in affluent areas.

Second, students in deprived areas, quickly realize they are wasting their time in a bad school and lose hope, leading to a downward spiral of underachievement and hopelessness, which feed on each other.

The underlying assumption which underpins the current system: *intellectual and attitudinal equality* is false. The result is that the country spends an astronomical amount of money to provide a mediocre service and to produce even poorer outcomes. And this is only going to get worse.

Under these circumstances, social mobility goes out of the window and so does productivity, as the pool of the educated becomes clogged with mediocrity, while the best are either held back in the good schools or completely wasted in the bad ones.

I do not believe that strict selection based on ability (innate intellectual, artistic or entrepreneurial ability, not homework, which is likely out of reach for children of deprived backgrounds and unappealing to budding artists or potential entrepreneurs) would be feasible in a Western democracy today. Actually, it may appeal to some, but it will not happen.

We have spent three centuries telling people that (1) a college degree is good for everyone, and (2) everyone has the intellectual wherewithal to attain and to productively employ such education. Both statements are false, but who would tell 95 percent of parents that their children would be infinitely better off not pursuing a route they have been told would be the best for them?

What we can do is make sure that the people who got us into this mess—the nationalized and heavily unionized educational establishment— are restricted in their ability to harm. The way to achieve this is to turn our schools, from kindergarten to colleges, into independent foundations designed to ensure the maximum level of participation of parents, teachers, alumni, and leading members of the community, and allowing free competition with for-profit providers.

The government should discharge its obligation to provide education by ensuring a standard payment for every student and an additional payment for those with disabilities, and by ensuring that all school-age children are in fact schooled. A regulatory framework and minimal bureaucracy to deal with inspections, complaints, and procedures should be designed to deal with failing institutions.

While not perfect, this will achieve several objectives:

- Empowering individual schools to tailor their offering to the needs, desires, aspirations, and abilities of the students
- Encouraging individual schools to specialize their offering—for example, a highly academic or a highly practical or a highly artistic or a highly entrepreneurial orientation, or combinations thereof
- Allowing at any given time the existence of a vast number of innovations in the field of education and comparing outcomes and establishing best practice
- Introducing cost awareness and a competitive culture
- Eliminating hundreds of thousands of bureaucratic roles, freeing resources for what really matters: the student
- Reducing the stranglehold of national or statewide teachers' unions and their one-party ideology
- Enabling ideological and cultural diversity to permeate this traditional bastion of the left
- Give parents and students a say in their own lives and futures
- Make education once again exciting and *progressive* in the true sense of the word
- Provide the economy with the entrepreneurs it needs, industry with the talent it needs, and society with the free citizens it needs to live long and prosper

I believe that anywhere between a third and two thirds of the funds employed by governments everywhere on education are spent on bureaucracy.

No centralization, no bureaucracy, and no uniformity. No bureaucracy and no uniformity means no waste.

MONEY, BANKING, AND CENTRAL BANKING

Centralization of credit in the hands of the state, by means of a national bank with state capital and an exclusive monopoly.

Karl Marx

MONEY

There are about as many definitions of money and currency as there are observers of economic phenomena. And they are all useful. Whatever people happen to use as a currency, from copper bars to pieces of gold, from olive oil to animal skins, a few characteristics can be observed:

- It will be used by many as a means of exchanging things.
- It may be used as a unit of account.
- It may be used as a store of purchasing power for the future.

Not all currencies display all of these characteristics. Not all classes in society have the same requirements in relation to currency. Not all societies will require (or be able to maintain) the same monetary arrangements. For most of human history, the household (whether a large estate or an independent farm) was a largely independent economic unit. Few people had much need or use for money, because few people needed to acquire what was not produced within the household.

Trade and finance existed, but only small segments in society were involved in them. The reason for this was simple: before modern agricultural methods and machinery, we needed about ninety-eight people working the land for every one hundred people in the general population. Vast numbers living in cities and lacking their own sources of food was a rare phenomenon before the modern industrial age.

The need for a currency fit for the modern age was pressing, and many individuals proposed alternatives. Various elements in society value (*value* meaning anything one seeks to acquire or retain) different aspects of the currency:

- Those individuals who rarely earn more than what they consume (low-paid workers) are largely interested in currency as a *means of exchange:* get paid, buy what you need, wait to get paid again.

- Those with well-established and regular sources of income (the state, large industrial and commercial enterprises, and so on) are interested in currency as a *means of exchange* and as a *unit of account* (information).
- Those who regularly produce more than they consume but do not "own" regular sources of income (well-paid workers, small businesses, professionals, and the like) are largely interested in the currency as a *store of purchasing power*.

It was only a matter of time before these separate and often inimical interests collided in a democratic state.

Hard metal, such as gold, is expensive to obtain, and it is a great store of purchasing power. But three quarters of the population will not have any left at the end of the month. *Workers* have little use for it. In industry, commerce, and finance, trillions of dollars change hands, but entrepreneurs are interested only in what to do with the profits. As long as the profits can be translated into a store of purchasing power or new investment, they are fine. The *business community* has little use for gold as currency.

Gold is undemocratic: politicians can successfully argue for the need to implement a program, but none of these arguments will conjure gold into existence. It will still have to be mined or taxed or borrowed or confiscated. The *state* has little use for it.

Once acquired, gold tends to retain its purchasing power, so there is a very limited need to "put it to work" by those who have earned it but have limited experience in or time for investing. *Financiers* have little use for it.

Only the lower middle class has any use for gold as a currency. And gold would reign supreme only for as long as the lower middle class held the balance of power in Britain in 1832–1928. After that, it would be a *brave new world*.

A stable currency—that is, one that holds its purchasing power over protracted periods—is apparently of no use to the masses, to the entrepreneurial class, or to the state. This is, however, a false assumption:

- When businesspeople and workers do not have to worry about the purchasing power of the currency, they can concentrate on doing what they are supposed to be doing: producing goods, providing services, creating jobs, and enjoying their lives.

- Planning and investments are fraught with uncertainty: a depreciating currency only adds more.
- The future production of goods, provision of services, and creation of jobs depends on investment, which is hindered by a depreciating currency.
- As investment is impeded by inflation, government revenues go down, employment goes down, and welfare dependency goes up.
- People's faith in the currency is worth many times more than any advantage to be had by debasing the currency to pay for expenditure.

Whatever definition of money or currency we employ, a truth remains: in its present form, it is absolutely pivotal in the maintenance and progress of our civilization. Gold will not be coming back as a currency any time soon; not a single individual in a position of power has any need or indeed desire for it.

If government spending is not kept in check, however, playing political games with the currency (QE I, QE II, QE III…QE ∞) will cost infinitely more than any temporary advantage that may be had by so doing.

The greatest beneficiaries of a healthy and stable currency system are workers and those on low incomes.

BANKING

Every time money is being accumulated where it is not likely to be used immediately, an opportunity arises to mediate between those who have money but will only need it at some point in the future and those who have actual or potentially profitable uses for it today.

Those bankers or financiers seeking to intermediate between cash holders (depositors, investors) and cash users (borrowers) will face particular challenges, such as not finding suitable uses for the money, the possibility that borrowers will not repay their debts in full when they fall due, that cash holders would demand their cash earlier than expected, and that governments would meddle in their affairs, among many others factors.

Moreover, banks can earn a living from only those who actually pay back. Bank clients will have to cover what the bank needs to pay those providing the funds (even the ones that will not be repaid) to compensate for the expenses incurred in the day-to-day running of the institution, to cover the losses originating from nonpayment, and so on. All this happens in a highly competitive environment.

The way to address some of these issues is to ensure the following:

- Capital. The difference between the amounts lent to borrowers and the amounts owed to depositors (and other creditors) should be sufficiently large to cover all expected losses and to remain solvent (or liquidated without a loss to depositors) after such losses have been incurred.

- Asset Quality. The assurances given by borrowers as to their ability and willingness to repay their debts when they fall due remain adequate and stable.

- Management. Individuals in charge of running the operation should be of the right caliber, education, and experience as well as adequately motivated and properly supervised.

- Earnings. What the lender charges its clients has to compensate for the cost of funding, the cost of capital, the cost of losses, and the cost of running the operation, among other things.

- Liquidity. In a modern setting, central banks are always ready to step in during a "run" or panic against a viable institution. The problem is that the general public never knows when an institution is viable or not. Banks require enough cash or cash equivalents at all times to ensure that any client that so chooses can withdraw her funds within a specified time frame.

Banking is not the easiest business to be in, but it's absolutely fundamental for the working of a healthy economy. Despite all these precautions, banks are commercial institutions that can and do run into difficulties.

Central Banking

When a banking institution runs into problems—either in reality or in the perception of the investing public—people rush to get their cash out before it's too late. Such "runs on the bank" can be very disruptive: a solvent institution can go under unnecessarily; depositors may choose to keep their funds at home; and if fear is widespread, it can lead to more institutions collapsing and further deterioration of the investment climate. Economic contraction and unemployment almost invariably follow.

The belief that a centralized system can avert unnecessary panic and the belief that having removed the panic element, banks should employ dramatically *less capital*—thus expanding lending and economic activity—*combined* with an almost dogmatic belief in the power of *state monopolies* to resolve all human problems led to the creation of the Federal Reserve about a century ago and most central banks around the world.

By any objective measure, the introduction of central banking as we know it has been catastrophic: never-ending recessions, never-ending depressions, global wars, misallocation of resources on a planetary scale, corruption on a planetary scale, and wholesale destruction of national economies. From the point of view of the professional politician or policymaker, things look much better. Pet projects are no longer limited by the need to tax or to borrow to defray their cost; they can simply print whatever amount they want without facing any kind of scrutiny.

In more senses than one, central banking as we know is deeply immoral, but it's *probably the only way to prevent overspending governments from literally employing violence to steal people's money.* The problem is the overspending, and the central bank has no means of stopping it.

Central banking enables the professional trade unionist to make and to obtain (and for the employer to grant) the most outlandish demands in the knowledge that the government will print the money to make it possible, at least for a while.

For the politically connected financier, the most adventurous behavior becomes acceptable, since in the case of crisis, the government will "monetize"—that is, will print the money they lost, make up the difference, and reflate the prices of whatever it was they had bought in the first place.

For the general public, the central-banking bag is mixed. Those on low and medium incomes suffer a constant deterioration of their earnings capacity (inflation makes the business environment more uncertain, thus reducing overall investment and, with it, the demand for workers) and a constant erosion in the value of whatever they have managed to save. For middle-to high-income workers, it all depends on their level of financial literacy. For retired people and others living on a fixed or largely fixed income, it's an unmitigated disaster: "the euthanasia of the rentier" Keynes so earnestly advocated. For welfare recipients it's again a mixed bag. Printing money enables politicians to dish out a lot more on entitlements than they would be able to tax from workers and business.

At the same time, the reduction of investment caused by inflationary policies means that once you fall in the welfare trap, you are unlikely to ever leave. As jobs become fewer and harder to come by, they will be increasingly reserved for those who do not normally require welfare payments.

What to do?

The heavy, progressive, or graduated income tax that Marx proposed to do away with the free world has been in place for three generations now. Every penny we produce is taxed and spent on whatever takes the government's fancy. If people manage to keep a little money after this fiscal onslaught, they are not in the mood for risking it on new and untried investments— the very investments employment depends on.

To prevent the economy from imploding for lack of investment (death by socialism) banks are requested to take risks they should never be exposed to. And, as if to balance the scales, when the resulting crisis hits, the central bank simply steals anywhere between one third to two thirds of the purchasing power of the money in people's pockets to make up the difference while socialist politicians blame *bankers* and *capitalists* for doing exactly what they were told they should do.

Marx knew what he was doing. The combination of a heavy progressive or graduated income tax with the centralization of credit in the hands of the state spelt the death sentence of the free economy upon which all our other freedoms depend.

I don't mind the tax being graduated as a practical matter, but as far the "heavy" part is concerned, *wake up, people!* This is a recipe for the destruction of the economy, not for a free, fair, and prosperous society.

Central banks have never been and will never be independent: our political realities make it impossible. Central banks can deliver neither inflation targets nor employment targets.

The only way to preserve the value of our savings and with them any hope of improvement for future generations –which can only stem from sound investments and not some government program– is to remove the temptation for the government to counterfeit the currency.

This can only be achieved by cutting the burden of the state back to size.

Only a taxation system designed to preserve the liberty and promote the prosperity of the nation –instead of some fabled redistribution of wealth– can achieve the goals we have set on our central banks.

Conclusion

Conservatism and Political Economy

Kirk told us,

> Almost from its beginnings, the Conservative party had been pitifully weak in its grasp of economics.
>
> Burke has possessed an admirable mastery of the subject and Pitt had understood finance; but except for Huskisson and Herries, from their times to the latter years of Salisbury's government, economists had been Liberals and the Liberals had trounced the Conservatives repeatedly in this field.
>
> As the old Liberals succumbed to the theories of socialism, the need for a conservative economics was desperate.

On that subject W. H. Mallock wrote in 1920,

> The difficulties in the way of formulating a true scientific conservatism, which the masses shall be able to comprehend, I am the last person to ignore.
>
> There is the difficulty of collecting and verifying the statistical and historical facts, to which general principles must be accommodated.
>
> There is the difficulty of bringing moral and social sentiments into harmony with objective conditions which no sentiments can permanently alter.
>
> There is the difficulty of transforming many analyses of fact into a synthesis moral and rational, by the light of which human beings can live; and feeling my way slowly, I now attempted to indicate what the nature of such a synthesis would be.

Kirk reminds us that Mallock was reduced to these lamentations after decades of meticulous study. He should not have bothered: liberalism, social-ism, National Socialism, communism, Keynesianism and welfarism didn't win the day because they were scientific, or even plausible. They were products of the imagination, and they appealed to the dominant feelings (and dominant constituencies) of their day: self-interest in the case of liberalism, envy in the case of socialism and communism, the helplessness of the Depression in the case of National Socialism and Keynesianism and the misguided humanitarianism that underpinned the welfare state.

The battle is for the hearts and minds; the science is always made up after the event. And made up science is impervious to evidence. In this age of equality, I would not dare to disparage these feelings; they belonged to a time and a place, and they are still strong among many. But neither should I feel ashamed of my feelings: I love my country, I love my people, I love the civilization that is my inheritance, I love the diversity that can exist only in individuality— all different, yet all *equal in our dignity*.

I love liberty, I love prosperity for me and my fellows, and I love enjoying my liberty under the laws of the land. This is what a thousand generations toiled for and several generations fought for.

I want everyone who so chooses to have a job or a business, to have a family, a house, children, cars, pets, peace of mind, and hope for their future and that of their children, their communities, and their countries.

A man's right to work as he will,
to spend what he earns,
to own property,
to have the state as servant, and not as master,
they are the essences of a free economy
and on that freedom all our other freedoms depend.

All this outpouring of emotion may sound extraordinarily vulgar to some. But you know what? I couldn't care less. And neither should you, or anybody else for that matter.

This outline of a *life worth living* is what conservatism is here to conserve and what the economics of conservatism are here to continue to make possible.

I cannot possibly fathom why I or anyone else should bow down to the person who claims that her feelings of envy or resentment—important as they are— should take precedence over everyone else's. We spent the nineteenth century forcing people to be free (and they became prosperous of their own accord) and the twentieth century taking away the freedoms we gave them and the prosperity they created.

In the process we have created a vast underclass, an even vaster bureaucracy, and a culture of victimhood and welfare dependency. We have failed the poor and vulnerable miserably; we have debased the currency; we have flaunted the Constitution and we have incurred astronomical amounts of debt.

Things can get worse, and they will if we don't stop the rot.

Despite Marx's and Keynes's best efforts, *liberty, prosperity, and the rule of law* are not yet repugnant in the eyes or our people; but they have no champion, and our nations are sleepwalking into a quagmire of stagnation and decay.

We need to muster the courage to free our people once again. We have done it in the past, and we have achieved wonders.

What are we waiting for?

REFLECTIONS ON THE "DISMAL SCIENCE"

Dividing economics into micro and macro, classical and Keynesian is highly misleading. What Karl Marx and J. M. Keynes called classical economy is the observation of the economic activities of a free and highly civilized society. It is the closest we will ever get to any true knowledge of political economy.

It is not true that classical economists dealt only with individuals and particular organizations. Far from it.

Marx, whom Keynes considered a classical economist, and Keynes himself, who is considered the father of macroeconomics, were political pamphleteers. Nothing in their writings can be even remotely described as scientific. Keynes didn't even pretend to be a scientist; Marx did. But only a "useful innocent" would call science what is in fact a gathering of carefully selected data to support a particular preconceived conclusion.

In another, more honest world, we would talk of the economics of plenty and the economics of scarcity, or more precisely the *economics freedom* and the *economics of slavery*.

The greatest achievement of our great liberal and socialist economists was to convince the world that they spoke for the science of economics and not from their political convictions and aspirations. The so-called macroeconomics is probably the most pernicious form of deceit, not only because it sounds compelling but also because—being the one that promises the richest job prospects for professional economists—it becomes a self-fulfilling prophesy. The more government control, the worse the economy performs; therefore, more government control (and professional economists) is needed in a never-ending spiral of stagnation and decay.

Each and every economic crisis of the past one hundred years has been caused by government action. The response from the civil service, the political class, and the economics profession has always been (1) to blame the crisis on not enough government action and (2) to propose more government action as only way to resolve the crisis, paving the way for the next crisis, in which the cycle is repeated with gusto.

MACROECONOMICS AND THE FALLACY OF AGGREGATION

Macroeconomists believe that, because they can aggregate something, that aggregation acquires meaning and can somehow be managed. It's like saying that if the United States has 304 million people and each has ten toes and ten fingers and 1.6 gallons of blood, the government somehow has an aggregate of just over three billion toes and three billion fingers, not to mention almost 500 million gallons of blood that need to be managed and balanced appropriately by several carefully coordinated government departments in consultation with state, municipal, and International FTB agencies (Finger, Toe, and Blood) and their legal and political advisers, professional lobbyists, and public relations agents.

THE EVOLUTION OF POLITICAL ECONOMY (WHAT WE NOW CALL "ECONOMICS")

As we understand it, economics came into being with Adam Smith before the first industrial revolution, therefore laying its philosophical and moral foundations firmly in the agricultural age. We moved slightly forward with David Ricardo, just after the start of the industrial age. Karl Marx decided to give up on freedom on the verge of the second industrial revolution, while John Maynard Keynes was active in what may come to be regarded as the peak of the industrial age in the "old" industrial world.

Given the time lag between the phenomena and the theories founded to explain them (and to guide future policy), every generation of economists finds itself applying policies devised for the previous age: classical liberalism (Smith and Ricardo) was as inadequate during the first industrial revolution as Marxism was during the second. Keynesianism was (and is) just as inadequate in the industrial as in the post-industrial age.

If progressive thinkers find themselves invariably behind the curve, just imagine how far behind conservatives are likely to be. We discovered classical liberalism in the 1980s and we seem to have discovered Marxism and Keynesianism in the small years of the third millennium (respectively 150 and 70 years after their authors, who were themselves talking for a bygone age). Burke effectively "founded" modern conservatism in 1791, so at the current rate, we may even discover *conservatism* in our lifetime.

REFLECTIONS ON POLITICS AND POLITICAL ECONOMY

There is no such thing as economics; there is only politics and behavioral finance.

The meaning of fairness was always summed up as "to each his own." Today it means "to each someone else's."

Humans yearn for good leadership. If they don't get it, they settle for *any* leadership. What they will never settle for is *management*.

From an early age, children learn that they get more from adults by saying, "I need," than by saying, "I want." And they never forget it.

Macroeconomics can be defined as the fallacy of aggregation.

A free society with a government monopoly on education won't remain free for long.

In *The Theory of Moral Sentiments*, Adam Smith told humans not only that they were good but also that they were naturally so. Humankind has not recovered from this delusion. Perhaps it never will.

"Society as a machine" may sound like a good idea, but as soon as the machine becomes aware of itself, it realizes that the best course of action is to switch itself off. That is exactly what we are doing at present.

The liberal belief system can be summed up as follows: This is what I believe, and once all evidence to the contrary has been silenced, suppressed, or destroyed, you will admit I'm right. Or else.

The most illiberal policies are sold as liberalism. This makes one wonder if the Trade Misrepresentation Act should also cover the world of ideas.

By the end of the nineteenth century, liberalism had gone from the champion of individualism and freedom to the champion of collectivism and control. True liberals came over to the conservatives. They brought with them their enthusiasm and ingenuity. Sadly, they also brought with them their self-doubt and their contradictions. Their enthusiasm and the ingenuity are long gone; their self-doubt and their contradictions are still with us.

People of moderate intelligence and learning are fascinated by the seemingly endless possibilities of state power. People of truly great or truly limited intelligence and learning are too busy living their lives. That is why politics is rarely done by the worst among us and even more rarely done by the best.

Over the course of five hundred years, the state has crushed the church with the help of the landowners, the landowners with the help of the industrialists, the industrialists with the help of the workers, the workers with the help of the bankers. Now the bankers are being crushed with the help of the free press. I can't imagine who will be next.

Marx proposed to do away with liberty, prosperity, and the rule of law, but failed to make them repugnant. Keynes was slightly more effective.

Keynes's *General Theory* is neither general nor a theory. It is a cleverly constructed devise to bring by stealth the system of slavery the communists had failed to implement by force.

Just like Marx, Keynes only speaks of labor and of "capital equipment." On the rare occasions when the entrepreneur is mentioned, it is always in the most derogatory manner.

"Schools of economics" tell children that they should have absolute power over their elders' pockets. Clever kids see through this nonsense, but clever kids don't become policymakers.

We cannot have checks and balances when all the levers of power are in the hands of the same trade union: The (Not Particularly) Worshipful Company of Politicians and Civil Servants.

Witch doctors of old promised to make a man or a country rich by wild incantations. Macroeconomists are their modern descendants, and they are just as effective.

Civil servants can easily become brutal masters.

Prosperity has no drawbacks, but all shortcuts to prosperity do.

Capital is *not* a collective product.

In ancient times, parents sacrificed their children to their gods in order to gain prosperity. Today they vote themselves entitlements that consume their children's hope of a future. Progress is not an illusion, but it is much slower than people imagine.

Edmund Burke's denunciation of aristocratic government as an "austere and insolent domination" is mildly amusing with the benefit of hindsight: the "government by shopkeepers" that came after him looked like an austere and insolent domination to the working class. Our modern quasi-dictatorships of the proletariat look like an austere and insolent domination to the Third World. In the eyes of those craving after someone else's power and money, *austere* means "not giving them your money," while *insolent* means "not recognizing their superior claim to it."

The question is not how many times or how hard we need to shuffle the cards to make them equal, but how much fun the game will be if and when we succeed.

The problem with idealism in politics occurs when ideas hit human flesh. Ideas are indestructible, humans are not.

True liberals appealed to reason and disappeared from history. Socialists appealed to feelings and are still going strong. Conservatives should learn this lesson.

The greatest threat to civilization is not property devoid of social duty but knowledge devoid of social responsibility.

We force everyone to live like the lower middle classes and call the outcome a classless society. How long before we silence all the dissenters and call the result a conflict-free society?

Burke knew and Kirk reminds us that economics and politics are not independent sciences. They are no more than manifestations of a general order, and that order is moral.

www.ingramcontent.com/pod-product-compliance
Lightning Source LLC
Chambersburg PA
CBHW070648290526
45790CB00001B/225